STAGING BREAST CANCER TRILOGY

Three plays
By
Catalina Florina Florescu, Ph.D.

NoPassport Press

Mia

Snowdrops and Chlorine

Cancer, Choreographed

By Catalina Florina Florescu, Ph.D.

Volume copyright, 2021.

All rights reserved.

For performance rights contact:

Author at fflorescu@pace.edu; Tel: 201-417-1577

Cover: *Untitled* (photography). Artist: Jamie Shombert (breast cancer survivor) Last photo: *Rodica* (personal archive).

NoPassport Press,

P.O. BOX 1786, South Gate, CA 90280. USA.
www.nopassport.org

ISBN: 978-1-6671-6133-4

Dedicated to my mother who introduced me to life and cancer.

Dedicated to Jo Spence, Audre Lorde, and all the men and women who some died because of, some survived breast cancer. I did *not* want to stay silent.

PREFACE

At the beginning of the 20th century, operating rooms were called surgery theaters because they were designed in such a way that, similar to people attending cultural events, those in the audience could observe the body being cut open, operated on, and sewn back. Moreover, at the end of these surgeries, people applauded. Imagine a sterile universe being humanized by people observing and learning. Imagine doctors being seen not as miraculous, mysterious forces, but as trained specialists. Imagine seeing the body without any clothes on -- its strength and fragility presented seamlessly before people's naked eyes.

Staging Breast Cancer Trilogy is a transnational, mixed-media project that continues and/or is derived from decades of research. In *Mia,* the first play from my trilogy, the focus is more on relationships and femininity. *Mia* had a staged reading in 2019 at LaGuardia Performing Arts Center and its world premiere has been rescheduled for fall of 2021at HERE: Arts Center (both directed by Handan Ozbilgin). In *Snowdrop and Chlorine*, the second play, I use more cancer-related terminology and I introduce a male character, as well as one real breast cancer survivor. The play was awarded an AFCN grant (the Romanian National Cultural Fund Association). The last play, *Cancer, Choreographed* is a dance based on a script (no spoken words) and in part it is inspired by letting the body *suggest* the pain and its healing process rather than verbalize it. After all, when in excruciating pain and terror, how often do we actually speak coherently?! It may help if we find someone to *dance* with.

In these plays, I observe how, regardless of gender, breast cancer breaks a body; how cosmetic surgery continues the job done by oncologists and how patients (may) have conflicting reactions about it; how the market is saturated with products "for" breasts; how information is sometimes manipulated and how isolation and lack of education and funds contribute to an accelerated decline in the recovery status of many patients.

Having lived for 2 decades as a hyphenated human (Romanian born, U.S. scholar), I am interested to notice how communities in Romania and the U.S. differ in their theatrical approaches to pain and management of information. Thus, I invite my global audiences to add their respective points of view. Moreover, techniques from well established schools, such as Theater for Social Change, Playback Theater, and Forum Theater can facilitate a discussion about empowering patients, as well as educate the medical community.

Lastly, I want all of us to *stop* assuming the body is a tool. The body is our home. Treat it with **love**.

MIA

MIA

In this play, three women talk about breast cancer from direct and indirect perspectives. A spouse, a doctor, and a school inspector are added to the plot. Who's in charge of our bodies? How do these women change, and what do they want us to change, too?

Script history

After I completed and published my first book, *Transacting Sites of the Liminal Bodily Spaces* (2011), catalogued at the Library of Congress, cited in the Oxford's Journal of the History of Medicine and Allied Sciences, archived in the Medical Humanities Dissertations and at the National Institute of Health, and part of prestigious national and international universities' collections, something was missing.

When I started my research, there was not one single play about breast cancer. There were memoirs, photos, and even a short film, but I wanted to read a play. I would finally find it, years and years after: *My Left Breast* by Susan Miller is a play who had its first performance in 1994, yet whose publication took place decades after.

I think I would have still written my own play even if I had the chance to read Miller's sooner. There was just too much love, anger, and information that I wanted to be out of me.

Industry praises

Mia tells the story of a breast cancer survivor as she rediscovers her own agency and self-identity following a mastectomy. The play offers a fresh perspective on cancer treatment, the process of recovery, the meaning of womanhood while navigating a male-centered and often misogynistic health care system. I had the pleasure of teaching the play last year (2019, A.N.), along with Catalina, in our honors theater course. Most of the students in the course were young women. The work inspired a very lively discussion while helping to dispel myths about what is mandatory for women to be "complete." We invited a speaker from the Going Flat Movement to also speak on alternatives to reconstructive surgery, which many of the students had not considered as even an option post mastectomy. The play has much potential as a tool to empower women with breast cancer, their families and support networks, as well as to raise awareness about screening and prevention — **Reginald Flowers**, Theater of the Oppressed Expert/Artistic Director of Falconworks Artist Group

With her Ionesco-like style, Catalina has expressed her characters' complex ways to deal with the pain and the betrayals of their own body, slipping into a sarcastic elevated word play to escape the confines of their body and self-image perpetually blasted and prescribed by the societal norms. What *Vagina Monologues* did for vaginas, *Mia* does for breasts. Catalina gave them a voice to speak of the silent suffering (of cancer violence), body oppression and their use and appearance being politically regulated – **Tjaša Ferme**, Artistic Director of Transforma Theater

In *Mia*, the author explores the way in which breast cancer shifts well-established notions of femininity and masculinity in a couple. Mia is a breast cancer survivor who discovers that being a woman who has lost a breast to cancer is the beginning of a new identity where she finds herself powerful, uncompromising, and beautiful. It is not an easy journey for her and her husband, who both discover how vulnerable their gender roles are. Through this play, the author alerts us to the fact that gender is a

construct that is in continuous transformation and definition – **Oana Chivoiu**, PhD, Assistant Professor South Louisiana Community College

I had the opportunity to read the play in its earlier stages, when as Co-Chair of the Ludics Seminar of the Mahindra Humanities Center, Harvard, I invited Dr. Catalina Florescu to give a talk on November 9, 2017. In her talk, "The Interplay of Ekphrastic Readings of Femininity Post-Mastectomy," Dr. Florescu presented her play *Mia* along with an innovative scrabble game she designed based on it, in order to advocate for cancer patients to have the final word on the method of their treatment. I admire Florescu's feminist approach to the issue of the coercive practices and discourses that affect women's self-image post-mastectomy. She is one of the scholars and artists who remind us that there is no right or wrong answer on these issues. There is only what is true to each one of the cancer patients. In every case, women should be offered full access to all options and decide for themselves regardless of any societal oppressive discourses – **Vassiliki Rapti**, PhD, Ludics Seminar, Harvard University

Characters:

MIA, professor of English, 36 years old, Eastern-European ancestry, naturalized American

MARK, bank executive, 39 years old, 4th generation American, very aware of his white male privilege

MEG, lawyer, 39 years old, Mia's sister, Eastern-European ancestry, U.S. resident

SAM, a tattoo artist, 25 years old, African American, and/or minority

An OB/GYN DOCTOR, 60 years old, walks and talks with authority, aware of his institutionalized power

A SCHOOL INSPECTOR, played by DOCTOR

Time:

The play commences in winter and ends in summer. Present time.

Place:

New York City.

Notes:

Lines in brackets suggest a character is self-censoring him/ herself (hence, that part is expressed nonverbally).

The protagonist, Mia, was diagnosed with cancer *by accident*. According to her doctor, a woman her age would not need to have a mammogram and/or an ultrasound recommended as part of her medical routine since (up to Meg's monologue) there was no medical history to trace the illness in the family. More, because she is under 40, her insurance would not cover the cost of a mammogram/an ultrasound either.

Meg's monologue is *not* an irrational intervention on her body. Her BRCA test reveals she has the faulty gene and has 90% chances to develop breast cancer. Until Meg does her BRCA test, neither sister knew that their grandmother had died because of breast cancer when she was in her early 40's. Their mother kept that a secret. That says a lot about how isolated we are when we are in pain. The play invites us to break this silence.

Acting:

Neither sister speaks with a heavy accent. Do not make that mistake when casting actresses.

Do *honor* their heritage as there is not one single type of English, but Englishes.

The three appendices should be directed offstage, suggesting how much each of these characters is willing to reveal about while accepting their limits and vulnerability. These appendices are also a way for us to think not only of breast cancer, but also of a way to use the characters introspectively, i.e., as a bridge into our own lives/bodies. We all want to be free, but paradoxically freedom is heavy; it may crush us if we can't be fully honest with ourselves.

Performance and beyond:

During the intermission, the audience members receive a questionnaire meant to be collected at the end of the play. The list of questions is revealed only during performance; if curious, feel free to contact the playwright. In addition to the questionnaire, one particular item of clothing will be added to further our understanding on/of femininity.

Maternity is a pressing subject for women, so read about "oncofertility," a term coined by Dr. Teresa Woodruff. Please take your time to decide if you want to become mothers. If you do, there are plenty of resources you can consult prior to starting your treatment for breast cancer.

Personal Note:

I was young and my body was developing when my mother told me she had breast cancer. I was the youngest in my family and the last to find out. We were not home, but in Bucharest because mother was doing chemotherapy sessions at the time. To say that I paid attention to the word, or that the word itself had any impact *in* the moment, that would be an understatement. It said nothing to me. It did not register. Skipping some seasons, we land in 1992. It's a "tsunami" of a year for me. That summer I am again alone with my mother: she plays maternally and covers her cancer majestically; I am a girl not fully in love, but definitely in search of it, or at least of the first serious kiss. We are again not home, but in Sinaia, a place famous for its royal Pelisor and its nearby Peles Castles, a place that reaches the 2000-meter altitude by riding a cable car, etc. To me, that summer is all about my mother's perfect way to hide her pain, something that I do not realize then, but only in retrospect. The same year, later in October, mother dies. She was 45 years old.

Skipping even more years, I am 35. My doctor tells me that I should start my preventive screening for cancer 10 years before the age when mother died. Because the system is built to ignore facts and the innumerable cases of cancer *diagnosed* at younger ages, I fight with the insurance and the hospital yearly. It's a "dance" to which I get more and more professional every year
because I am sick and tired of hearing that "I am too young to develop breast cancer." Cancer is not like one of those rides at an amusement park where if you do not have the recommended height you can't get in. Cancer is a **beast**!

For 5 years I have this "dance" with bills that I decline to pay because they are unjustified. I always win. But that's hardly my goal in facing this complex of illnesses. I meet women who have been diagnosed with breast cancer, I listen to their stories & carefully archive them inside my body, I am very aware of the fluctuations within and outside of the medical communities, and I am determined to speak up. It's not that I am a rebel per se, it's rather my stubbornness to admit defeat and/or accept that I can't have a say in this illness. We all do, whether we are healthy or sick, free to roam the streets, or confined in hospital beds—or, really, *in between*.

Mia is a play that helps me advocate for health and respect. During the intermission, the audience participates in a questionnaire that leads to something else. We should *not* have one month dedicated to awareness. We should *not* even listen to anything these corporations may claim to do for breast cancer. This type of effort is just a scratch, not a deep bleed, the way we truly feel about the illness and its costs. Wear or not wear the pink ribbon, that's not for me to decide, but find out who represents your voice in Congress, reach out to that Office, and demand ways to make the screening for breast cancer affordable regardless of age and family history. Demand the costs for treatments to be significantly lowered. I have met and/or heard of too many GoFundMe campaigns or, worse, bankruptcy stories because of the piling costs of this illness. Ask these corporations that keep wasting money on products to switch their focus and to invest in the treatments' costs and preventive screens. More, stop denying a patient's agency to accept or deny reconstruction after mastectomy. Use Amendment 9, the most generous of all given its openness to seek changes: "The enumeration in the Constitution, of certain rights, shall not be construed to deny or disparage others retained by the people." If we have desensitized re: breast cancer that is in direct relationship to having been flooded by pink and not a serious talk. We walk the walk, but we do not march directly into the above-mentioned offices. We wear a ribbon, but we do not look at the scars. We cover up. *Why* do we do that? Why do we return home and wait for another October?! People suffer physically, emotionally, and financially. When are we going to act like adults?!

When my mother told me she had breast cancer, we were standing in a way that would *mark* me forever. She did not choose it that way. It just happened that at the moment of "I have to tell you something. I have cancer," between a mother and her daughter there was *a bed*. Instead of a hug, we looked at each other in silence. I was lost. She was lost. Ever since that moment, I have been breaking down the layered silence with which breast cancer has been swaddled. *Reciprocate*!

Act 1
Scene 1

The décor is simple to indicate a desire to enlarge the living room, to make it breathable. De-cluttered. Alive. On a table, a selection of organic fruit, vegetables, and spices are still in their original package. To intensify the emphasis placed on the word organic, directors may take three to five brown paper bags and write on each of them in uppercase letters: ORGANIC PEARS, ORGANIC CINNAMON, etc. Mia sits by a computer. She wears a black robe. She sings along with Etta James' "At Last." She sings for a minute or so. When Mark enters, we hear clearly "... and life is like a song." Then Mia sees Mark at the door, about to enter, panting.

MIA (*Only to the audience*): Uggggggh, this one! Look at him. (*She mimics his panting mockingly*)

    MARK *enters.*

MIA (*To him*): I read that those who jog die, too, honey.

MARK: Die *happy.*

    He leaves the room. Offstage: "Craaaaaaaaaaaaaaaaaaap!" He enters the room, half naked, with a minuscule towel covering his intimate area.

MARK: The shower broke???

MIA (*Nods*): I wanted to replace it myself, but, instead, I bought these ... (*Points to some bags which are randomly placed on a table and/or on the floor*)

    No answer.

MARK [What the hell?]: So, what, should I stay covered in my sweat all night?

MIA: It's either that, or you could wait a few more months to get your driver's license back and replace the shower yourself.

MARK: Some option...

MIA: Are you hungry? Try some organic celery.

> MARK *exits. Offstage:* 'Fuuuuuuuuuuuuuuuuck!" MARK *reenters. He is angry.*

MARK: Where the fuck are my clothes?

MIA: I dropped them off by the cleaners. They were dirty.

MARK: All of them???

MIA: Yes.

MARK (*Very rapid switch, lovingly*): Ooooooh, I get it. Am I your love toy tonight, my queen? (*Winks and bends*)

MIA: I've lost my crown.

MARK [I'll be damned]: What's your game?

MIA (*Blunt*): Your clothes will be cleaned professionally – that's all.

MARK: That doesn't make any sense.

MIA [If we could switch bodies]: Our bedroom is cold.

> *An awkward pause.*

MARK: It hurts, dear, I know (*she mouths silently pointing to her chest and then down at the belly*) yeah, of course, *you* hurt, but that's no reason why you should hurt other people.

MIA: Whom am I hurting?

MARK (*Raises his voice*): Mia, it's maddening! Adopt a pet. Help orphanages. Do something. *Anything!*

> *In his agitated speech, he drops the towel. This creates a short hilarious moment that manages to break the tension between* MARK *and* MIA. *We see* MARK's *behind.*

MARK: What the hell, is this a kitchen towel???

MIA: Yeah, manually embroidered. (*Gets closer. Moves around* MARK's *body*) Look at the tiny flowers, dragonflies, and butterflies. Look at the pastel colors. Where could Thumbelina be?

MARK: Are you ... high... drunk?

MIA: Let me grab my camera. (*Takes a few shots*)

MARK: Jesus, are you *done*?! When they said intimacy, they meant something else, not this invasion, or (*getting closer*) is this your foreplay?

MIA: One more shot. (*Takes the last shot and then turns the camera off*)

MARK (*Sits on a couch*): Good, you're done. (*Pause. Finds a throw blanket and covers himself a little bit more*) How was your day?

MIA: My sister called. She wants to visit.

MARK (*Not enthused*): Great.

MIA: I told her we'd go on a cruise.

MARK: Huh?!?

MIA: She reminds me of a time when I didn't even know I had a body.

MARK [*I am tired!*]: Look, Mia, it's not your sister's fault you can't keep a pregnancy. Or that you had cancer. (*Tries to fix his bluntness*) Never lose hope.

> MARK *tries to make* MIA *stop what she's about to do. She is even more determined and stands up. First, she faces only him.*

MIA (*Loud and powerful*): Look at me! (*Half of her robe is at her waistline*)

> MARK *stands up and tries to make her put the robe fully back on.*

MIA: No, thank you.

> MIA *turns herself to face us. We discover a big, ugly, real scar on her left breast.*

MIA (*With anger and disappointment; only to the audience*): I want to take my insides off, throw them, 'cause they've already betrayed me, and put cotton balls inside me. You know, the same way they make stuffed animals.

> MARK *finds a bag full of cotton balls on the couch.*
>
> *Examines them.*

MIA (*Grabs the bag*): I've been looking for these all day yesterday.

MARK: For...?

MIA: A project.

MARK: You are full of secrets today.

MIA: If you must know, I was imagining I was a doll. Dolls don't have nipples.

MARK: Yeah?!

MIA (*Repeats what she shared with the audience earlier*): I want to take my insides off, throw them, 'cause they've already betrayed me, and put cotton balls inside me. You know, the same way they make stuffed animals. (*Dreamingly,*): I feel like I said that before.

MARK: Said ... what?

MIA: Cotton balls, cotton balls, balls, balls, *balls* inside me!

MARK (*Consoling*): You'd make a perfect stuffed animal. (*Beat*) You still look good to me.

MIA (*Clears her voice*): Still is such a revealing adverb: "Hey, you can't walk like you used to? Don't worry, what matters is that you're still alive." (*Touches her scar*): "Hey, you lost a boob? You still... you still..." (*Does not know how to finish*)

MARK: Mia, honey, calm down.

MIA: Who, me? Ever since *you* discovered that mole on your right cheek, you barely touch that spot when you shave.

MARK: Hospitals are scary. All those long corridors, neon lights...

MIA: Vitamins and antioxidants to make us stronger and healthier. Don't people know that, many times, we improve one element in a system, and another may collapse? Fix the transmission and the carburetor may break... It's very simple: shit happens (*with emphasis*), pain happens.

MARK (*Claps*): That's a very elaborate theory. Should we call a medical journal?

MIA (*Points to her scar*): They say when you lose a hand, a leg, or a breast, you're still able to somehow feel them; you have the phantom limb experience.

MARK: Sounds like a fairytale.

MIA: It sounds so fascinating (*faking excitement*), a phantom in your body (*blunt*), but it's not. Because you are not you anymore. There are ghosts inside your body, crawling, itching, eating you alive. (*Change in tone, now neutral*) Anyway, I don't feel my lost breast at all, as if it never existed.

MARK: *I* find you attractive, but you reject me and, lately, you don't even want to have sex, even if our doctor said that "...continued, frequent intimacy..."

MIA: "... may result in a pregnancy." (*Firm*): I live with you, but fantasize about the one I fell in love with sixteen years ago. (*Goes closer to him and says this line very sensually*): I have a daily affair with a former you. (*Switches back to normal*) Or maybe I'm just waiting to find the perfect lover to have an affair, who knows?

MARK: All this talk about lovers, cotton balls, and... Wanna go to bed?

MIA: Nope.

> MARK *kisses* MIA *on her head and exits.*

MIA (*Goes to her computer; starts typing*): What happened today? What happened today? (*Scrolls, nods, etc. Stops. In shock*): Noooooooooooooo! Nooooooooo! She was only 40!!! And had three kids. Fuck, no. Nooooooooo! (*Will you allow the woman to cry? After a moment, standing up,*): Laurie was a UPS driver. She is the most optimist person I have ever met. She was.

Was??? Fuck. No, that can't be true. She lo- (*tries to say the verb, but hesitates between present and past*) loved blue. When I first met her, I thought all that blue was too much: her nails were blue, her hair was blue, her shoes were blue. I asked her why that color and she said, "Have you seen us patrolling in our uniforms? We look like soldiers delivering ounces of pretend happiness. Soldiers? Well, I don't know. Maybe I have a thing for them." She laughed and pinched me. She asked me about my fantasy. I said I was married. She said that I needed one right away. "Get a lover, dear, life is short and fucked up." When I was with her, that cancer ward was full of life; she listened to music and let me borrow one of her headphones. We laughed and danced. We made plans to go on a bullet train ride in Japan to see how everything would pass us by so, so, (*getting emotional*) rapidly. Now she's dead. (*Reads with disappointment from the screen*): "She's survived by her kids." How the fuck are those surviving without their mother? Ughhhhhhh. (*Walks very upset, maybe stumbles onto something*): Cancer, *ugh*!

She exits. Offstage: "Mark??? Mark?"

There is a smooth transition from dim light to dimmer to darkness. Complete silence. Then the lights return and MARK *sits down in* MIA*'s place.* MARK *stands up and looks at the audience.*

MARK: *Who* can sleep in this agonizing silence? When I rest my head on a pillow, I think: am I still a man? Should I assert my masculinity by speaking in a more convincing way? Should I tell Mia she is too bitter? Nah, she'd kill me. Should I howl at the moon? No, that's a wolf's job. Should I mark my territory in the apartment by peeing? No, that's a dog's fun activity. Ever since Mia's diagnosis, three years ago, I've felt less and less like a man. When she was finally cancer free, things got even *worse*. I couldn't offer her what she wanted: a child. I couldn't help her "fulfill" herself "as a woman." Not my words, hers.

MIA, *still offstage*: "Mark? Did you go out *again*? It's late for jogging."

MARK (*Stage whispers*): I *don't* sleep anymore. I go there, in our bedroom, but stay awake. I sleep in the office between meetings. But I need to tell her. There is no way I should keep avoiding telling her (*after a pause*), the truth. It's the only thing that would break this dreadful silence and put me to sleep.

He leaves on his tiptoes. On a screen, random words should be seen in a very rapid succession: "femininity," "cancer," "maternity," "marriage," "pressures," "identity," and "meanings." The last word gets increasingly bigger until it drops off of the screen and it is replaced by "definitions." When the word "definitions" is projected, a light travels on stage until it illuminates a door, as if behind that space there is this very orderly, artificial place where definitions are stored in unopened boxes. That moment will help transition from Mia and Mark, the couple from the first scene, into a dream-like sequence.

Scene 1

Appendix

When the door opens, we see a row of chairs resembling a classroom. Mark is the only one who is seated. Mark wears a uniform or pajamas that look like uniform. He is playful and very aware of himself as a student. Mia holds a grade book. She appears to be confident, but in reality, she's a mess. Still, they both render the rigidity and the expectations imposed by their social roles.

MIA (*To the audience*): Did you ever read these (*skeptical*) classics? *The Capital* by Karl Marx? (*Drops it*) *Discipline and Punish* by Michel Foucault? (*Drops it*) *Madame Bovary* by

Gustave Flaubert? (*Drops it*) Uggggghhhh, this one... it's in all hotels. Care to guess? Yep, *The Holy* freaking *Bible* by .... Anonymous. (*Winks*) By white men. Who else had access to education back then? (*Wants to drop it, too, but instead picks up all the other three books. Checks herself and enters*)

MIA: Good afternoon. Today it's an important lecture. I shall speak about our roles in society. (*Even drier than before,*): We, humans, build a society. Let's pretend these books are some bricks and we want to build... (*Starts to build*)

MARK (*Interrupting to get her attention*): Hey, teacher, build without *a* foundation?

MIA: The foundation exists. And don't you *ever* interrupt me unless you want to be punished and disciplined and sent into the Principal's Panopticon! I mean Office. (*Still standing up and continuing to build,*) This first brick represents all of us. We all have a contribution in society. And we also have a distinct role. Let's not forget the chaos that happened in the Babel Tower. We need to agree on one language and speak that until we die. We cannot let confusion ruin our lives. We must also understand that our roles are fixed and not interchangeable. It's quite simple. (*Slowly, she becomes incoherent and that will be reflected in her speech, more and more, like in a dream, unreal*): A man's role is to be the head of a family and ... provide for his family. A woman's role ... is ... to give birth .... and take ... care ... of her ... children. A society prospers when ... when... when...

> She collapses. As her body weakens while falling, she destroys the construction.

MIA: Fuck... all of this!

> A SCHOOL INSPECTOR *enters. He sees the teacher on the floor, but disregards her. Although he's definitely uncomfortable in his tight school uniform, he never*

admits it verbally; only his body suggests his discomfort.

A SCHOOL INSPECTOR (*To the student in the classroom*): What happened here? (*Does not let him answer. Facing the audience,*): Doesn't matter. I need to visit 10 more schools today and deliver the same speech. (*Clears his voice. His whole speech and attitude should signify pettiness, yet magnified grandiose gestures. He is a mess, too, but will never admit that verbally. Starts with the same speech as* MIA's)*:* Good afternoon. Today it's an important lecture. I shall speak about our roles in society. (*Even drier than before,*) We, humans, build a society. Let's pretend these books are some bricks and we want to build... (*Starts to build*)

MARK: Excuse me, sir...

A SCHOOL INSPECTOR (*Surprised*): What?!

MARK: What's your name, sir?

A SCHOOL INSPECTOR: Boy, be quiet! I don't have time to waste. (*Trying to find his last words as if they were floating in the air; he says the following mostly to himself, stage whispering*): Where was I...? What was I saying? (*Satisfied, clears his voice. With confidence,*): There are only two genders: male and female. A woman's role is procreation and protection of her family. A man's role is to go to work. My role is to make sure the curriculum does not change. We need to keep students contained. We do not need a revolution. All big changes bring chaos and after that we have to reestablish order. Why bother when all we need has already been presented to us? Why wouldn't we want to live a happy, quiet life?

MARK (*Finally paying attention*): Sir, sir... (*Coughs*) Mr. teacher, sir, could you please say it louder? I have a bad ear infection. (*At that moment takes a pencil and starts to write down feverishly*)

A SCHOOL INSPECTOR: We should ...

MARK: Repeat the last line, please.

A SCHOOL INSPECTOR (*Flustered, but keeping his masked cool*): It is our duty to ensure kids learn what *we* tell them it's important. (*Looks back through his papers and repeats what he said before, getting more frustrated with the tightness of this clothes*): There are only two genders: male and female. A woman's role is procreation and protection of her family. A man's role is to go to work. My role is to make sure the curriculum does not change. We need to keep students contained. (*Intense eye-contact with the student*): Remember this: learning is fun. Now you say it.

MARK: Learning is fun.

> *Before he leaves, he rearranges the construction erected by the teacher. Leaves the stage indicating he might take his uniform off. He can barely walk, and he is visibly frustrated.* MARK *puts his head on the desk. The light from the beginning of this scene may return to travel onto the stage as it pleases. Projected, we read: "A woman's role is procreation and..." Instead of reading the line in full, that is erased completely. "A woman's role is ..." That gets erased, too. "A woman is..." This remains unfinished because we hear a bell ringing, and that could be an alarm clock.*

Scene 2

It's morning. Mia brews coffee. She wears silky red pajamas. Mark enters wearing a short floral kimono and cowboy boots. The contrasting elements in his attire are deliberately funny. He stumbles as he walks. We hear James Brown's "It's a Man's, Man's World." Mia sings happily, even if a little bit off-key "... but it would be nothing, nothing, without a woman," when, suddenly, loud sounds are heard. Mia has dropped all of her pans.

MARK: Damn it! I can't walk in these anymore. (*Seeing the mess with the pans*) What *carnage* just happened here?

MIA: Look at you, so dressed up.

    MARK *bows. Then he points to the pans.*

MIA: It's an installation.

MARK: You *don't* even cook.

MIA: Nothing gets stuck on these pans.

MARK: What are you even *talking* about?

MIA: Don't you know about the revolutionary Teflon?

MARK: I know about the American Revolutionary War.

MIA: *Lame.* (*Beat*) They came up with this amazing thing called Teflon: no trace left behind!

MARK [Another joke, I see]: So, you want to experiment with disappearance...

MIA: Yes, and launch a new segment on the Food Network Channel: Transcendentalism and Teflon: A Revolution at a Woman's Fingertips.

MARK: David Copperfield cooks (*winks*), maybe?

MIA: *Pass.* Neither Houdini nor Copperfield is invited in my pants. Oops, I mean pans. (*Seeing what he wears for the first time,*): Are those your old college boots?

MARK [Yeah, baby!]: Last time I wore them I felt like a stud.

MIA: You always looked ridiculous in them.

MARK: Let's agree to disagree.

MIA: When you bought them at the flea market, you said you'd hope to have fun. Did you?

MARK: Plenty, in my dreams.

> *Awkward pause.* MIA *offers him a cup of coffee.*

MARK: Thank you.

MIA: Speaking of dreams, I was jumping off of our bed *naked*, all sweaty, and was calling you.

MARK: Go on. (*Invites her to dance, but there is no music*)

MIA: Let me speak.

MARK: Go on. (*Arranges his kimono to deflect the tension*)

MIA: I was naked, but you were sitting apathetically on our living room couch and ... (*looks at his face which has changed from excitement to disinterest*) ... and as I entered the room, you *completely* ignored me.

MARK: Who, me? This? (*Incredulous*): Me??? (*All this time he points to his body as a clear indication of his secured metrosexuality*)

> *While he turns his back,*

MIA (*To the audience*): Men's confidence in their bodies is really something, isn't it? They are not born with it. They find it all around them. (*Adds*): *Effortlessly!*

MARK (*Turns his body to* MIA): Did you say something, honey?

MIA: No.

MARK: That was all? With the dream?

MIA: Yes, Mark, that was all (*with emphasis*) *in* the dream.

MIA (*To the audience*): This nakedness. In my dream... I was *me* ... the other version when cancer was not part of my life. (*Sighs*)

MARK (*Completely unaware of her confession*): There, I found it.

MIA: What?

MARK: The button. I don't want to parade here naked.

MIA: Since when do *you* have a problem with that?

MARK: Since yesterday when you took those photos of me.

MIA: You know... Never mind.

MARK: What now?

MIA: In my dream...

MARK: You said it was over.

MIA: The dream, yes. But it *bothered* me.

MARK: Let it go.

MIA: No!

MARK: Suit yourself.

MIA: Let's talk. We never talk.

MARK: Fine, talk.

MIA: When I came naked and you ignored me, it felt like we

were the two characters in these paintings. (*Points to two reproductions of Edward Hopper's "Excursion into Philosophy" and "A Woman in the Sun"*) It *didn't* feel like a dream.

MARK: What?

MIA: These! (*Shows him the posters*) Why did we buy them?

MARK: I dunno... weren't we at our university's book fair ... or something?

    MIA *nods*.

MARK: We were students, young, penniless, free.

MIA: ...and in love.

MARK: Madly. (*Continuing his previous thought,*): We were, I think, about to leave when you noticed a room full with posters. You spent ten minutes examining *Les* (*babbling*) *De- de- moise-lles* ... (*Scratches his head as a mnemonic device; no result*)

MIA (*Adding,*): ... d'Avignon. (*Says is again fully and with authority*): Les Demoiselle d'Avignon.

    MARK *applauds with arrogance*.

MIA: I thought those women were caught in a sticky trance and, at the same time, ready, alert for hunting: those hungry eyes, those ridiculously rigid postures. (*Starts imitating them as she moves closer to him*) I thought those women were converted to hunters. They looked like Diana, but they didn't need to carry a bow and arrows. They had the *possessed*, intimidating look: it was enough if they stared, and you'd become their instant victim. No bloodshed. *Fascinating*.

MARK: Scary. (*Takes her hand so she could feel the goosebumps on his forearms*)

MIA: I know, I know, *baby*, that painting has always intimidated you. *Womanists* should have used it more often. We have finally escaped the male jungle.

MARK (*Adding with satisfaction,*): ... and entered your own. (*Howls*)

MIA (*Puts his hand over his mouth*): Why didn't we buy the Picasso's poster?

MARK: Don't ask me.

MIA: You were the only one with me that day. Try harder!

MARK: You said something about... about... (*not sure*) hunting?!

MIA: Yeah, I had you.

MARK: Exactly, you didn't want to hunt anymore because you wanted to (*becomes more sensual*) devour me.

> *There's a fleeting intimate moment between them. It almost feels they are about to rip their clothes off. Maybe that even happens. She loosens up. She is playful.*

MARK: I *adored* your giggle. It was one of the reasons why I fell in love with you...

MIA (*To the audience*): *Fell* in love? *Adored*? *Was*? All in the past? Did I die? And he gets to live?

> *A moment.*

MIA: Be frank...

MARK (*Interrupts her*): I can't be *Frank*. I'm Joe. (*No response*) You used to laugh at these silly remarks.

MIA: Why did we buy those posters instead?

MARK (*Wants to answer quickly and be done with this memory*): Weren't you fascinated by the naked woman?

MIA: I was???

    MARK *raises his shoulders.*

MIA: We've had these posters for so many years, but I never dreamt that I was that woman until last night.

MARK: Why bother with what happened in a dream?

MIA: Why, indeed! Do you want another cup of coffee?

MARK: No, thanks. Is there something to eat?

MIA: Try some dried organic prunes. (*Hands him a bag*)

MARK: These are loaded with dietary fiber, which makes them an ideal laxative. Go figure discussing the economic meltdown and global recession when, all of a sudden, I'd need to be excused for going to the restroom every five minutes.

MIA: I forgot businessmen don't know how to crack a smile. When they do, it feels like they are recovering from a Botox treatment. C'mon, Mark, you can't deny that the economy is so destructively funny.

MARK: In that case, I'll speak with the Director of our Human Resources. Maybe we could hire you to teach a workshop on "Introduction to Laughter and Deficit Markets," "How Laughter Could Make You Disregard Your Empty Bank Account," "You Don't Have Money to Pay Your Mortgage? Laugh out Loud!"

MIA: I miss teaching comedy. We are all so *deadly* serious today. (*Pause*)

MARK: Now, *you* could eat plenty of dried prunes. I've noticed a stack full of papers.

MIA: I'm terrified to start grading.

MARK: Then give them fewer assignments.

MIA: It's much easier to kiss a frog and turn it into a prince than to change those *dinosaurs'* mentality who are in charge with the curriculum.

MARK: But students could think through performance, role-play.

MIA [Tell me something I don't know!]

MARK: *Fuck* curriculum! Remember their age, Mia. When you were nineteen, you were drinking and partying a lot. You didn't care about your education. Being a teenager is all about balancing your hormones. It's like a daily invitation to Woodstock.

MIA: Actually, I partied that much when I was nineteen because my parents left me to figure out what it meant to fail on my own...

MARK: You had *perfect* parents.

MIA: How would I know?

MARK: Teaching is like parenting.

MIA: Not even close.

MARK: If I were your student, you'd fail me.

MIA: Let's see.

MARK: What?? I was *not* serious.

MIA: Shhhhh. Let's play.

MARK: In the bedroom? Nah, it's fine right here. Facing those goddamn posters.

MIA: I can't have sex with my students.

MARK (*Playful*): But, teacher, I am over 21. Plus, you are *really* horny.

MIA: My game, my rules.

MARK: Fine.

MIA: How'd you define freedom?

MARK: If I answer incorrectly, will you spank me?

MIA: Answer! (*Wants to undress him*)

MARK (*Startled a little bit*): What ... was .... the question?

MIA: Define freedom!

MARK: Freedom means (*...somewhat turned on*) ... going to a store dressed in a kimono and wearing boots.

MIA (*Her desire to undress him stops*): Huh?!?

MARK: It's not casual Friday, and, even if it were, I'd never cut for a believable *geisha*.

MIA (*Realizing he is serious,*): I could offer you a ride.

MARK: Nah, I'm fine. Pete is going to pick me up.

MIA: What would he say about your (*emphasis*) feminine attire?

MARK: I thought *you* wanted me to start a clean life... this is why you (*makes air quotes*) dropped off all of my clothes, right, dear?

MIA (*Concerned*): What about those people at the store? Will you *at least* wait in the car?

MARK: Last time I checked this *was* the United States. It's a free country. Besides, what could they do? Arrest me for being dressed in a kimono? That would be politically incorrect. I'll be fine.

> *He plants a kiss on her head. They both exit the stage in opposite directions. Before she exits, she stops and looks at the two posters.*

ACT 2

Scene 1

Winter has gone. Mia waters plants and sings lovely tunes. She wears a white suit. The skirt is short to reveal her beautiful body. She wears make up. We can hear Annie Lennox, "Walking on Broken Glass." She appears ecstatic. Mark looks at her with love.

MARK: Wow, sexy. Bought a new dress?

MIA: I am making myself a dress.

MARK: Nice!

MIA: One day I was putting my uniform on, old jeans and a black sweater, when I had an epiphany: *who* the hell is that *dead* woman? I felt chills throughout my body. I ran away from the mirror and searched for my measuring tape. I went to a store, bought a colorful fabric, and started cutting and sewing. (*Tries the unfinished dress on top of her suit*) How do I look?

MARK: Alive! (*Kisses her*)

> *She takes his hands and puts them close to her torso. She opens her hands wide, and he does a check-up, emphasizing the breast and underarm area. He stops. She touches her belly.*

MIA: Aaaah, I almost forgot... My sister is coming this week. She stays with us for ten days. Maybe I'd design her a dress. It's distractingly relaxing to touch a fabric *imagining* the contours of one's body.

MARK (*Checks his phone*): Ah, there it is... We are going to the doctor this week.

MIA: Not *we*, Meg and I. Besides, you have to build that crib (*points to a large, unopened box*).

MARK (*Distracted*): Yeah... I need to order some tools.

MIA: So, order them! (*Touches her belly*): *This* time it'll be better.

She exits. He picks up his phone. Sits on the box.

MARK: Hi, Pete. What's up, man? Wanna do something this Wednesday morning? Golfing? Tennis? (*Taps on the box*) Eleven, perfect!

John Coltrane's "Equinox" starts playing.

Scene 2

An OB/GYN office. On walls, there are various images of gestational uteruses. For a contrasting note, in the background, it would be effective to have some mirrors that distort one's reflections, just like in a children's museum/amusement park. Mia and Meg exchange looks. Like an aural membrane from the previous scene, Coltrane's song is still playing. We never "bring" a silent body, do we? Then, the song fades away.

DOCTOR: Good to see you again, Mia. How have you been feeling?

MIA: *Growing.* Glowing.

DOCTOR (*No emotion*): I'm happy for you. (*Invites her to sit on the examination table. Turns the ultrasound's screen on. Long silence. Takes off his gloves*): It's empty. I'm terribly sorry.

The next scene happens as if MIA *was invisible.*

MEG: Doctor, that *can't* be true! She hasn't had her period for the past eight weeks!

DOCTOR (*Precipitated*): We'll conduct some immediate tests, request them urgently, do our best. (*Wants to leave*)

MEG (*Grabs him by his left arm*): Enough with this defensive medicine talk! Besides, we waited for 30 minutes, you examined Mia for two, but the bill will be ridiculous. Now, do you want to leave us *agonizing* what could be wrong?

DOCTOR: It could be anything, from a persistent cold to cancer. I wouldn't rule out early menopause.

MEG: *Menopause*?! Meno...? What?! Hell, *no*! She is too young.

DOCTOR: There're recorded cases of menopausal women in their 30's.

MEG: *If* it's menopause, could we... (*Beat*) What could we do?

DOCTOR: We'll seek the ideal treatment. I'll let her oncologist know immediately. But first we need to identify the cause. Order blood tests. We need to be very cautious; cancer could be in remission, or have a late, aggressive effect. Cancer is perverse.

MEG: A *war* is perverse. Cancer is *unnecessary*. Unbelievable!

> MIA *sits up and starts touching the images with pregnant uteruses, then, she moves in front of the mirrors, which distort her bodily contours. She is successively smaller, then taller, fatter, and thinner. Then she imagines her body being pregnant. Touches her imaginary pregnant belly with affection. Her hands migrate toward her lost breast. She is devastated. The actress should show/embody this devastation. She turns away from the mirrors. When she talks, her sister and the doctor seem to be in a trance.*

MIA (*To the audience*): Wanna know the truth? I haven't felt like a woman lately. After my breast cancer diagnosis, I have been like a sleepwalker on a tight rope, not knowing where I'm going, or when my body will betray me *again*. (*Beat*) I have never liked periods but, nonetheless, there is something fascinating about them. For one thing, they flow... they are warm and life-like... they are soiled and life-like... they are cyclical and life-like. (*Starts to move towards the doctor and her sister and, the closer she gets to them, the more they seem to return to life, unfreeze*) A part of me thought I was pregnant. I've gained an inch or two around my waist. I know that because I've designed a dress. I did *not* dream that. No, no, *no*, it was real. (*Looks directly into the doctor's eyes*) Is this even a doctor's office, or is it a place where dreams are crushed? (*She seems to be falling, but her sister catches her. They are one body now*)

DOCTOR (*Tries to be sympathetic, yet he is too technical and rather detached from the situation, speaks very slowly, as if explaining English to a foreigner. He is too loud and very irritating*): De-ar Mi-a, so-me-ti-mes we ga-in a fe-w pou-nds with-out a chan-ge in o-ur di-et. Th-at is pa- rt of o-ur fluc-tu-a-ting me-ta-bo-lism. We fe-el sen-sa-tions th-at a-re not ac-tu-al-ly ha-ppe-ni ing be-cau-se of o-ur i-ma-gi-na-tion or (*back to normal*) autosuggestion.

> *During the doctor's detached, arrogant speech, we see how both women get increasingly and rightly so frustrated. The change from* MIA's *vulnerable moment is going to reverse to her typical tough way of being.*

MIA: Are you having a *stroke*? Meg, call 911. We are losing this male doctor. (*Different tone*): Oops, we are in a hospital. (*She points to a copy of Rembrandt's "The Anatomy Lesson"*)

DOCTOR: I am sorry, I didn't mean to...

MIA: Our bodies rule over us and we can't control them or even predict their next move. [You act as if we *just* met] I *know* this. I've experienced this, remember, because I had a little bit of...

fuck, what is its name? Oh, yes (*very clearly*), breast *cancer*!

> *The two exchange glances and are quite displeased to be in the same room. They move towards the copy of the painting with* MIA *in the lead, followed by* DOCTOR, *who is symbolically tied on a leash.* MIA *points to this man, and that man, and the other man in the painting, and then, as a Q.E.D., to the male doctor in the room. While* MIA *does this,*

MEG (*To the audience*): When I first heard the word cancer, Mia was like a statue. I had to shake her. Then, I was so sorry. (*Beat*) It's funny, isn't it? We answered the question of the Sphinx, but we didn't get her enigma. The full, undisclosed test wasn't who walks on four, two, and three legs, but that we're a bundle of cells full of *random* choices and chances.

> MEG *looks around. Gets closer to* DOCTOR.

DOCTOR [These two!]: I'm sorry, I can't answer *all* of your concerns. I am *only* a doctor. Your oncologist should be contacted. STAT. Right now, Mia, the important thing is to rest.

MIA (*Now is her turn to speak very slowly*): I d-o n-ot fe-el ti-red. I a-m di-sa-ppoin-ted. Wh-at co-uld yo-u pre-scri-be fo-r (*back to normal*) disappointment?

DOCTOR: When it rains, we open an umbrella, or we seek shelter. There's the same algorithm with an illness: we try to get as much love and support as possible. No one likes to get wet. But sometimes it rains.

MIA (*To her sister*): Isn't he funny? (*To him*): There are no tests or drugs for *disappointment*. That's the bottom line. Although, paradoxically, it has a damaging side effect: chronic bitterness with periodic episodes of *self*-punishment.

DOCTOR (*Exasperated*): I *really* must go. I have other

appointments.

MIA: Hurry, *please*. Tell them that joke with the umbrella. They'll shit their pants laughing. *What*, is shit a tough word for you? (*More to herself*): Scatology and oncology.

DOCTOR: The nurse will give you some brochures on your way out. (*Heavy habit*): Have a great day!

MIA (*Facing the audience,*): Great... *what*?! "Have a great day???" My body is a mess! Ah, we are trapped by these civilized mechanical reflexes. We can't mourn publicly the loss of our healthy bodies... FUCK! What can you do with a body that is out of sync? The ill body is a burden. A load too much to carry *only* on our own. But we prefer to be silent when we suffer... we feel extra bad or something. (*A pause*) I feel that I need to do something that I've never done in my life: give up. Wow, I got chills just saying that. (*Tries again to "test" the realness of what she says*): Give up! Yes, yes! (*With confidence*): I will *never* become a mother. My left breast is *forever* gone. They say hope dies last. But what happens (*shows this with her hands*) when you hold hope so *tight*, you don't even realize when it has managed to slip away? (*A pause*) I was going to teach my class when I got *the* call. That day they were assigned to read Ibsen's *A Doll's House*. I entered the classroom. They were talking. They were laughing. They were absorbed in their phones. I sensed their youth as if then and there I had seen them for the first time. Mid-session, someone tells me I had a stain on my shirt. I looked and realized I was holding my marker on my blouse, next to my breast. I stained it. I wanted to laugh. But instead, I went to the bathroom. I saw my ruined blouse. No one was there. I yelled. The janitor came. He asked if everything was fine. I couldn't say a word. He gave me a bottle of vodka. "Here???" He said: "How could I otherwise deal with this mess?!" (*Beat*) I can't remember anything else that day. But I kept the stained blouse. It was marked by an accident in my body I had no idea how to fix.

For a few seconds, there is no one on stage. Then we hear Scene 2, Act 1 or Montagues and Capulets fight from Sergei Prokofiev's "Romeo and Juliet." The whole scene is visually submerged in Rembrandt's "The Anatomy Lesson." The scene ends with a light show that reflects the unspoken tension between DOCTOR, *on the one hand, and the two sisters, on the other hand.* MIA *and* MEG *dance together to suggest oneness.* DOCTOR *is pushed back. Again, there is no one on stage. The music still plays. Then* MARK *pushes* DOCTOR *back onto the stage.*

Scene II

Appendix

DOCTOR: Look, what isn't clear? I told them *all* they needed to know. Everything will be fine.

MARK: Everything will be *fucking* fine?! How much more do I have to wait, doc?

DOCTOR: Just a little.

MARK: Fuck, I can't.

DOCTOR: It's tough.

MARK: Listen, one dude to another. I'm ready.

DOCTOR: For?

MARK: A vasectomy.

DOCTOR: Huh?!

MARK: I can't give Mia the child she desperately wants.

DOCTOR: It's not your fault. It's cancer's. Or she's menopausal.

MARK: I *don't* give a fuck whose fault it is. I don't want kids. I mean, if they come, they come, but if you have to work this hard to have a child, then fuck it.

DOCTOR: Stop this. I have work to do. How can I help, *really?*

MARK: With a vasectomy. I *already* told you.

DOCTOR: Christ, are you out of your goddamn mind?

MARK: I've never been *more* lucid.

DOCTOR (*Casually, about to leave*): I am not a urologist!

MARK: You graduated medical school. That's *all* I care.

DOCTOR: Leave!

MARK: *You* know our past and you're the only one who can help me.

DOCTOR: Are you drunk?

MARK: Mind your fucking business!

DOCTOR: It's *my* office.

    MARK *takes out a knife.*

MARK: Look, Doctor-Pussy, if you don't take this seriously, you're going to bleed like a bitch. I order you to do it. I want this to be *over.*

DOCTOR: I need a nurse, an anesthesiologist, and a signed agreement.

MARK: You need shit. It's just the two of us. Or else... (*Points to the knife)*

> *We hear some sounds as if a knife cuts through various things, each with distinct consistency. Imagine you cut an apple on a cut board. The sound may continue as we move to the next scene. There is this almost seamless impression of cutting something that manages to crawl under our skin.*

Scene 3

A retro, chic café. When Mia and Meg enter, we hear P!nk's "Try."

MIA (*Sings repeating the last line, "Tell me, are you just getting by? You gotta get up and try and try and try"*): This is my favorite place.

MEG: This is the first time when you take me here. Must be special.

MIA: Yes, I am in the mood to celebrate.

MEG: What?

MIA: My body is an asshole.

MEG (*Not sure if MIA is intentionally funny or not*): Your body is an ... asshole.

MIA: Yep.

MEG (*Trying to change the subject*): This place reminds me of Europe. It has that air, doesn't it?

MIA: Yeah? (*Raises her shoulders*) They make the most delicious Irish coffee. We ask the barista to make it *stronger*. (*Winks*)

MEG: It's eleven in the morning. I don't feel like drinking.

MIA: Well, *I* do. My body just handed me another blow.

MEG: And a drink will help?

MIA: Not really, it's not magical, but I'd like to try something new. A memorial of sorts...

MEG: Who died???

MIA: Duh, my body.

MEG: Let's go home. You are weird.

MIA: No!

MEG: Maybe ... go for a walk?

MIA: If you don't want to stay, *don't*! I want to drink!

MEG: Fine.

MIA (*Rather abrupt*): Why the fuck do I obsess about a pregnancy?

MEG (*Half-voice*): Have you ever considered adoption or surrogacy?

MIA: Surrogacy??? I did not freeze my eggs. Cancer did not contact me, "Woman, do something with your eggs 'cause in a few months' time I am gonna really fuck up your whole life."

MEG: And adoption?

MIA: How do you decide which child is worth adopting? Isn't that cruel? It's not like choosing a spouse...

They both giggle.

MEG: Look, you've tried getting pregnant; you did not freeze your eggs; perhaps you should look into adoption.

MIA (*To a waiter, indicating she knows him*): Tom, my usual. Make two Irish coffees, I want to initiate my sister in the (*smiles*) exilir vitae.

MEG: I don't want to drink.

MIA: *Pleeeaaase*.

MEG: Just one drink.

MIA: Sure, one. (*Winks*)

MEG: I'm serious.

MIA: Noted.

MEG: So, adoption? Will you give it a chance?

MIA: What am I, a kid, who can't do things by herself?!

MEG: Bullshit! I can't do my gardening. So, I hired a gardener.

MIA: Oh, yeah, Jesús. I wish I had a garden... I have this apartment in the city. We are all breathing each other's recycled sighs, farts, and insecurities. (*Faint smile*) I'm jealous. You have that big house and that beautiful garden. I wish I had that. Then, I could borrow Jesús; you know, I have my own bushes. (*Laughs*)

MEG: I'm sure he could help you with that.

    They both laugh.

MIA: This Irish coffee, didn't I tell you? Panacea. (*Half-turning her body*): Tom, could I please have another one? Just make sure you put more whisky and almost no coffee this time, OK? (*To MEG*): I read an interesting article the other day. It appears that modern science has been attempting to cure depression with Deep Brain Stimulation.

MEG: Are you depressed?

MIA: Shouldn't I ...?

MEG: What did the article say?

MIA: They insert a pacemaker in your brain that sends stimuli throughout your body. It's nice to hear of any scientific progress.

MEG: You know so many things about the human body.

MIA: They don't teach much of this stuff in high school. We learn formulas, how to *never* put a comma between a subject and its verb, we read the classics, of course, a little bit of chemistry just so we know about oxygen and hydrogen, but we do not learn anything about the human body. Ah, wait a minute, I almost forgot: we do learn, *zoology*, about frogs and how to dissect them. Now, seriously, when am I going to dissect a frog? We discover our bodies once they are broken, and that's embarrassing.

MEG: Maybe it's protective. We find out the truth only when it's *absolutely* necessary; like when we were kids and believed in Santa Claus. Hey, do you remember when we played that librarian game?

MIA (*Pleasantly surprised*): Yeah. We removed all the books from the shelves, and then we pretended to welcome people in to borrow books. That *wasn't* a traditional children's game.

MEG: You know...

MIA: What?

MEG: Nah,...

MIA: If you have something to say, say it!

MEG: I hated that librarian game!

MIA: What??? I don't believe you!

MEG: I haaaaaaaaated it!

MIA: You never told me.

MEG: Did you feel protected among those books, or what?

MIA: Protected??

MEG: The game invariably ended with me running after you. You pretended to be lost in its imaginary corridors. Maybe I didn't like it because I was jealous.

MIA: Of...?

MEG: Your imagination.

MIA (*Plain tone*): About those imaginary corridors...

MEG: Yeah?

MIA: You are wrong. I wanted to run.

MEG (*Annoyed*): You *hated* running! In fact, when we were outside, at a park, you never ran, not even when it rained. You said, "It's just a rain. It'll pass." (*Softer, lovingly*): You were an original child. I don't know why you deny *yourself* that.

MIA: How so?

MEG: Many times, after we played our silly librarian game, I was *so* bored with those books, I needed air. You, though, remained there enraptured, putting the books back on the shelves.

MIA (*Blunt*): I didn't want mom to yell.

MEG (*Frustrated*): You were mom's *favorite*! She adored you. I *had* to get sick to receive her attention. *Even* then she brought you along.

    The tension between sisters escalates.

MIA: *You* dragged me along.

MEG: *Bullshit*, mom took you! I wanted to be alone with her. But no, *you* had to come.

MIA: *If* you claim so…

MEG: Arrrgh… I need a punching pillow when I'm with you.

MIA: Like you are so easygoing. (*Scoffs*)

MEG (*More composed*): Look, do you find some kind of pleasure telling lies to yourself, or are you completely disconnected from your past?

MIA (*Finally vulnerable*): I *don't* know. Shouldn't I hate my … (*will she say "myself"?*) past?

MEG: No!

MIA: But I was whole then.

MEG: Look, maybe that's your real problem: some sort of unidentifiable amnesia. (*Realizes she does not want to hurt* MIA) Damn, they make a good Irish coffee! (*Sips*) Listen, you don't need to get pregnant to identify who you are. I'm not a mother. That's fine. Not all women should become mothers.

MIA (*Totally lost, showing her increased vulnerability; addressing this twice, once to her sister, then to the audience*): Then who the fuck am I? *What am I?* (*Hides her face*)

MEG: You are *hurt*. Deeply. I know. (*Hugs her*) Your body is a war zone. But ... (*trying to find the right soothing words,*): ... but ...

> At this moment, a large woman enters in the café with some flyers. She greets Tom, the waiter. She is very friendly and polite.

SAM: Hi.

MEG: Yes??

SAM: I'm sorry, I don't mean to interrupt.

MEG: Can I help you with something?

SAM: I'm not lost.

MEG: Then?

SAM: May I have a minute of your time?

MEG: We are kind of in the middle of something... (*pointing to* MIA) Sorry.

SAM: Sure.

> SAM *starts to leave. As she leaves, she drops some fliers.* MIA *picks one up.*

MIA: Excuse me...?

SAM: Yes?

MIA: What are these?

SAM: I do tattoos.

MIA (*To* MEG): Let's get tattoos!

MEG: What's with you today?

MIA: I don't know. (*To* SAM): What do you think?

SAM: Well...I'm the best.

MEG: What??

SAM (*With confidence*): I'm the best.

MEG (*To* MIA): What would you get?

MIA: A haiku. (*Ab-lib, counting the syllables*):

Can-cer, can-cer: breast,

You give milk, you give me death.

It is ... (*Stumbles*) it is... Fuck, I lost my train of thought.

SAM: ...blindingly.

MIA: Huh?!

SAM: Blindingly!

MIA: Oh, yeah, it fits! Meg, what do you say?

Can-cer, can-cer: breast,

You give milk, you give me death.

It is blindingly.

MEG: It does not make *any* sense!

SAM (*Pulls up a chair*): May I?

MEG: Oh, my God, yes, please.

MIA: Maybe I should do something else with my life.

MEG: What's happening today??

MIA: Listen, I became a professor driven by the desire to inspire others. But when I discovered that I couldn't teach myself how to loosen up, how to care less, how to live what is meant to live, I felt betrayed. (*Says it one more time to make sure* MEG *gets it*) Betrayed by *myself.*

>SAM *realizes that she should not be part of this conversation. Stands up.*

SAM: I gotta go. If you decide to get a tattoo, the number is there.

MIA (*To* SAM): Maybe you are Godsend.

SAM: Nah, I'm just a single mother tryin' to pay my bills.

MIA: God works in mysterious ways.

MEG: Stop!

MIA: What?

MEG: Let's not freak out this woman.

MIA: Fuck, not another lecture on God.

SAM: God?! (*Scoffs*) God is an invention.

MIA: Amen!

MEG: I guess you found your *sister.*

SAM (*Playfully*): Godsend.

MIA: Maybe that's a sign.

MEG: For...?

MIA: For starters, the Apocalypse.

SAM: Another lie.

MIA: Amen! Listen, when I was doing my chemo, I had to escape some place. When Laurie was with me, it was fine. But when she was not there... Those fluorescent lights, those linoleum floors, those IV poles, those motivational posters... pink everywhere. Did I tell you?

MEG: Tell me what?

MIA: One day, after a chemo session, I went home. Mark had to pick me up, but he called last minute and said there was a crisis on the market. I said, *Don't bother, the global economy is dying. I am fine*. I called a Uber and the guy was so young. He kept looking at me in the mirror, and I said, *Yes? Do I have my shirt unbuttoned? Never mind. There's nothing here you want to see.* I started to cry. He pulled over. I thought he would rape me. Those sick things you hear on TV, all Uber drivers are rapists, so, anyway, he opened the door, came next to me, and hugged me. That stranger did that and then I cried even harder. I think I cried all my tears that day. I said I wanted to go home and take a shower. He said, *Fine*, and went back to his seat. But before he did that, he looked in his pockets and took out a lollipop. He gave me that, and I said, *Thank you*. It was pink. It was in the shape of a ribbon. I started to laugh hysterically. The man probably thought I was a lunatic. He said, *What's so funny?* And I said, *Nothing. Just drive*. Pink ribbons and pink lollipops to cure cancer. Ridiculous! (*Silence*) Sometimes, I fantasize quitting being a professor, going to a bank, applying for a loan, finding a cozy place to rent... Sometimes... (*Beat*) (*To* MEG): Wanna do something together?

MEG: Get a ... tattoo?

MIA: Nope, something else.

MEG (*Exhausted*): Jesus! What now?

MIA (*Somewhat witty*): Start a business.

MEG: She (*points to* SAM) is not a magician. This morning I woke up a lawyer. Can't turn into something else just like that. (*Snaps her fingers.* (*To* SAM): I'm sorry, what's your name?

SAM: Sam.

MEG: I'm Meg, and this is my little sister, Mia. And apparently, we forgot our manners.

SAM: I should've said my name.

MEG: Mia, if you want to get a tattoo, I'd need some time. Sorry, Sam. I can't commit right now.

SAM: No problem. I gotta go to pick up my kids from school.

MEG: Sam, let's stay in touch.

SAM: OK. (*Starts to exit*)

MIA: "... my little sister, Mia." Sounds like I'm spoiled.

SAM: Did you say something?

MIA: To my sister... I will call you, Sam.

MEG: And you are not?

MIA: Spoiled?

MEG: Fuck, Meg, maybe cancer did make me act like a brat.

MEG: Don't *play* stupid. I mean as in ... entitled.

MIA: You are, too.

MEG: Yes.

MIA: Seriously, do you want to do something together?

MEG: If I answer, could we *pleaaaaaaaase* leave this place?

MIA: Let's open a library-café! No clocks, microwave, or anything even remotely touched by technology. Just people and fiction.

MEG (*Practical, wants to be over with this*): Fine!

MIA: You mean it?

MEG: Wait a second… How would you make coffee?

MIA (*Ecstatic*): I'd make Turkish coffee. And I'd serve some snacks. People would read. People would talk. (*Smiles*) Never mind. You hated that game when we were kids.

MEG (*Raises her cup of coffee,*): I'm in. To your library-café!

MIA (*Beside herself, maybe the happiest we have seen her so far*): You, sure-*sure*? You couldn't commit to a tattoo just seconds ago.

MEG: That's a permanent mark. Your library-café would be a safe space for people and (*emphasis*) fiction.

> *Throughout the intermission when the questionnaire activity occurs, we listen to Nina Simone's "Don't Let Me Be Misunderstood and Edith Piaf's "No, je ne regrette rien."*

ACT 3

Scene 1

MEG (*To the audience*): Mia will kill me if she catches me doing this. Maybe it's silly. It's hard to explain. (*Beat*) I mean, really, what do you do when you are lost? When you lost something dear? *Someone* dear... (*Sighs*) Our parents were atheists. But our grandpa was very religious. He loved to do what I do right now. I caught him once. I was a teenager. I made fun of him. "How would holy water do miracles?" And grandpa said it did *not*. I was in shock. How many of us do something even though there is no promise of remedy? But there's *comfort*. When our father died... nothing helped. Until I remembered what grandpa used to do. There is no sure thing to fixing pain and longing.

> When MIA *enters,* MEG *has just finished her monologue to the audience and is in a totally blissful moment. She is at peace.*

MIA (*Loud*): Meg??

MEG (*Startled*): What???

> MEG *drops the holy water bottle.* MIA *picks it up.*

MIA (*Ironic, but mean*): Try Kombucha.

MEG: What??

MIA: If you want to drink something new.

MEG: Too bubbly.

MIA (*Suspicious*): What were you doing?

MEG: Nothing.

MIA: I don't believe you.

MEG: You don't believe *in* anything.

MIA: True.

MEG (*Matter of fact*): Calm down. I was *just* blessing your walls.

MIA: The fuck!

MEG: Look, I thought that blessing your walls with holy water would keep bad spirits away.

MIA: Are you out of your mind?! What bad spirits? Wouldn't be easier to jump off of a window every single time something bad happened and we wouldn't want to confront it?

MEG: My dear, you're not practical.

MIA: And *that*'s your concern? We aren't primitive people to think malevolent spirits still exist among us. (*Scoffs*)

> *The tension between them grows. But it's needed to push outside whatever is not yet fully ejected. It is so much different than the tension between* MIA *and* MARK, *or* MIA *and* DOCTOR.

MEG: Then, how do *you* explain all calamities? What is so unthinkably bad to connect with your religion?

MIA: To answer your first question, if something bad happens, it happens. When a tornado comes, you don't kneel and pray; you run away as fast as you can, like a professional athlete aiming for the Olympic gold. Your second question proves that *you* are not practical. To each their own God.

MEG: There is only one God.

MIA: *No, no, no!* But you know what, that's not even the point! You came to help *me.*

MEG: What do you mean, that I should help you in a *prescriptive* way?

MIA: Maybe I am not Christian Orthodox anymore, but Buddhist. Just because I was baptized that does not mean I shouldn't change my religion. I am a free person.

MEG: You should've told me you changed your religion. I would've understood. I'm not *that* narrow-minded.

MIA: You should've asked.

MEG: Really, Mia, *really*?

MIA: Here you are, under my roof, doing things only a priest should be doing. By the way, where did you get holy water?

MEG: You could get it on Sunday <u>if</u> you attend Mass. (*Making fun of her sister*) Or buy it from a supermarket.

MIA: Huh?! Are you telling me that *I* could buy holy water from the same place where I buy eggs and toilet paper?

MEG: *Sure.* There's a whole aisle dedicated to all things Christian.

MIA (*Acting pretend-stupefied, otherwise she is fully aware she is mocked*): Which aisle, before or after the Crusades?

MEG: Household stuff: zip locks, detergents, mice traps... *Don't* make that face. We are obsessed with sanitizing and keeping everything nice and neat.

MIA: What face? So, wait a second, could anyone *play* priest?

MEG: I am *not* playing priest; I am just anointing your walls.

MIA: I forbid it!

MEG: I'm a religious neophyte myself.

MIA: What?!

MEG: You don't know the word?

>MIA *nods that she does.*

MEG: When daddy died, and you did not bother to pick up the phone, the only comfort that I could possibly find was in God. I prayed and prayed night and day, day and night; then, I started to anoint the walls of my house until I felt I wasn't alone in my suffering any longer. I was protected and finally at peace with my once tormented soul.

MIA: Basically, you found a shortcut.

MEG: It's ironic how you, a professor, can't accept that progress relies on self-education and emancipation, and that suffering should be taken out of one's body. We can't ask God for anything, except maybe for peace. The moment when you discover that inner peace and elevated tranquility, you notice that all bad things pass you by. (*Mimes while speaking*) Your body becomes a rowboat and your arms your oars with which you swim farther and farther... (*Opens her eyes*) What *bliss*! You literally feel your body like a vehicle that transports you toward an unknown realm.

MIA: I see... and Charon is taking us to Hades.

MEG (*Ignoring*): Let's try together.

>MEG *puts her hands on her sister's shoulders.* MIA *rejects that gesture.*

MIA: Leave me *alone*! God, Meg, you make me feel horrible, like I'm possessed. [Jesus, just because I don't go to church... never mind, I don't want to finish this spiraling-good-for-nothing thought]

MEG: *Why* did you invite me here? I'm terribly sorry you're so stubborn to accept change. Sometimes I wonder if you perhaps find some kind of devilish pleasure tormenting you and the ones who love you.

MIA: Once a body breaks, there is *no* going back, no matter what you and your loved ones want to believe. *Humpty-Dumpty* all over again, this time for real. Once a piece falls, all the others fall, too. *Domino*. And not the game. Ever since my diagnosis, I've been taking naked pictures. You know... as mementos. I don't need blessed walls. *Or* God.

MEG: How could you fight with a concept? It's a lost battle!

MIA: I'm a concept, too; an (*emphasis*) embodied concept. (*Beat*) My body is a war zone, do remember what you said before?

MEG: Let's get some fresh air.

MIA: Yes, let me grab my sneakers. Wanna stop by that café?

MEG: *No*, thank you. How often do you go there?

MIA: Don't worry, that's just as effective as your holy water.

MEG (*Lovingly,*): Shut up!

Scene 2

Mia and Meg enter accompanied by Sam. Mia gestures casually indicating "Feel at home." Mia drops her purse carelessly.

MIA: Let me grab my robe and we'd start right away.

    SAM *nods*. MIA *exits*.

MEG: You know, that day at the café...

SAM: Yeah...?

MEG: I never asked...

SAM: What?

MEG: How did you become a tattoo artist?

    MIA *enters*.

SAM: Didn't have a choice.

MIA: What did I miss?

SAM: Nothing. I was telling your sister about my job.

MIA: I see.

SAM: Before this, I worked at "Beauty within"... within my ass. Oops. (*A pause*) My body was not like this.

MEG: You look fine.

SAM (*Not convinced*): Thanks? I was size zero.

MIA (*Doubtful*): You don't say...

SAM: You should have seen your faces. (*A pause*) I was fired once I got fat.

MEG: You need a lawyer.

SAM: Can't afford.

MEG: Pro bono?

SAM: It's too late.

MEG: Retroactive benefits.

SAM: I got better things to do.

MIA: I like your attitude.

SAM: Mia, you sure about that tattoo? Once I start, that's it.

MIA: Let's do it!

SAM points to the couch.

MIA: So, you are a mother, right?

SAM: Yep.

MIA: How many?

SAM: Three. In vitro fucked my body. Nobody said shit to me.

MIA: What are you talking about?

SAM: I wasn't like this. I was skinny.

MIA: What happened exactly?

MEG: *Mia!*

MIA: *What?!* Why are women *so* afraid to open up?

SAM: I like to talk. (*Sees the scar; reacts*): I grew up alone... Grandma said women in her family gave birth to many children. My mother had some complications with her pregnancy. Plus, my (*ironic*) daddy never showed up.

MIA: You never met him?

SAM: Nope. Could be anyone.

MIA: I'm sorry.

SAM: I'm not. I grew up with two strong women.

MEG: Our mother was tough.

MIA: Well, ...

MEG: Well, *what*???

MIA: Not today. We have company.

SAM: See, that's what I miss.

MEG: The bickering?

SAM: To have a sister. Or a brother. Someone to talk to.

MIA: I'm sorry.

SAM: Do you say that a lot?

MEG: Not even once to me. (*A sharp look at* MIA)

SAM: Did you fight a lot?

MEG: We still do.

SAM: Cool.

MEG: Exhausting.

MIA: Like you are some kind of prize!

SAM: Awesome, man!

MEG: I'm glad you like our (*makes air quotes*) show.

MIA: Maybe that's what we should do.

MEG: Huh?!

MIA: Have our own reality show.

SAM: I'm alone. My husband said he would never fuck a pig.

MIA: He must have been prince charming.

SAM: The bastard fries everything, so his arteries would eventually blow up.

MEG: *Sue* the bastard. I'm sorry.

SAM: What's with you two? What's with the apologies? I thought my kids would grow up to know their father, but he ran away like a son of a bitch he is. Is yours any good?

MEG: They are from a catalogue.

SAM: What??

MEG: Never mind.

MIA: What's that? (*Pointing to* SAM's *tattoo*)

SAM: After I got fired, I was so scared... no partner, three kids. I thought mine would end up in that awful foster care system... so, I took online tattoo classes. I'm certified. Look, (*pulls up her sleeve; reads in a dignified voice*): "Lost body to *in vitro*."

MIA: Sam, can I ask you something?

SAM: Yeah.

MIA: Are you happy as a mother?

SAM: Happy? Hm... I get tired easily... I'm taking care of triplets. Some neighbors help. I take them to the tattoo parlor. It's hard. You know,...

MIA: Yes?

SAM: Women like me *don't* think about happiness.

MEG: My sister and I obsess about it.

SAM: Funny, right?

MIA: What?

SAM: How we speak the same language, oh, well, almost, but we say different things. (*Beat*) There're days when I can barely breathe, tie my shoelaces, or even sleep comfortably. (*A tad hesitantly,*) You had cancer, right?

MIA: Yes.

SAM: I *fucking* hate cancer. My mom died because of breast cancer..

MEG: I'm sorry. I *really* mean it.

MIA: Well, ...

SAM: Look, you took it out. You are *alive*. My mother said it would pass.

MEG: Pass??

SAM: She thought cancer would pass... like a cold. She didn't want surgery. She kept massaging it, made her own lotions, stunk up the place, and nothing... the bastard grew bigger and bigger. My mother had ...

MEG: Are you OK?

SAM: My mother's breast had HOLES... cancer perforated her skin, and she was *still* making lotions!

MIA: Don't be so hard on yourself. Some women can't accept to lose their breasts.

SAM: Why the fuck not?! These boobs are *not* mandatory.

MEG: The stupid social echo.

SAM: Never heard of that.

MEG: It's all around us, like air.

MIA: But polluted.

MEG: Non-breathable.

SAM: Slow down, I don't follow.

MIA: Women are pushed to get reconstructive surgery. Who the fuck wants intruders in their bodies?

SAM (*Finally joining the sisters,*): The *silent* killer.

MEG: Amen!

MIA: *Fuck* this social echo! Bodies break. End of story. *Fin*. Roll the credits.

SAM: You have residues of anger. (*Determined, with emphasis*): I just can't deal with women fighting with themselves. Don't we have *enough* to put up with?

MEG: True.

SAM (*To* MIA): Go look in a mirror. You chose a bold tattoo, "Dignity."

   MARK *enters*.

MARK: What the hell is going on?

MIA: Sam, meet my husband. Mark, meet my friend, Sam.

   MIA *invites* MARK *to shake hands with* SAM.

MIA (*To* MARK): That scar was too *standard*. Now I have one breast and one "Dignity." (*Points to it*)

MARK: I see, you didn't ask for my permission.

MIA: I am *not* ten!

SAM: Permission?? That's *her* body, dude.

MARK (*To* SAM): I'm talking to *my* wife. (*To* MIA): I thought we were a team...

MIA: Do you want a tattoo?

MARK: Not in a million years! The needles may be infected.

SAM: Watch it, buddy!

MIA: You and your paranoid obsession. Whatever... Meg, it's your turn.

MARK (*To* MEG): I thought you were rational.

MEG: "Girls" just wanna have fun, Mark.

SAM: Yeah, Mark, wanna have fun?

    MARK *ignores* SAM.

MIA (*To* MEG): What are you getting?

MEG: A purple cross.

MARK: You've lost your minds completely!

MIA: Sam is also a psychic and could read your future. Tempted?

MARK (*Yells while he exits*): No!

SAM: Am not.

MIA: Mark's scared of *anything* new.

SAM: Now that you mentioned it, I could've been... (*Takes her phone from her back pocket, scrolls, stops. Gives the phone to MEG*): Read this.

MEG: "Want to get a better job? Choose from these must-have qualifications: Anti-Freudian psychic reader, voodoo nutritionist with penis envy, monogamy interpreter with self-designed damnation rings, vegan stylist guru, cuckold trainer with candy sucking fixation, shibari post-secondary school for educators."

All women burst into laughter.

MIA: To think that all these years I've been teaching the *wrong* subjects. (*Laughs*)

SAM: You a teacher?

MIA: More like retiring.

MEG: Shall I be sitting on the couch?

SAM: Yes. Let me wash my hands first.

MIA: Sam, when you're done, do you want to stay for dinner?

SAM: Sure.

MIA: I have these Teflon pans.

SAM (*Doesn't know what to say*): Good for you.

MIA: We could cook together.

SAM: Awesome! I haven't done that in years!

MEG: This is out of the blue. Sam, my sister and I aren't that good.

MIA: Speak for yourself. I am terrible! (*Smiles*)

SAM: I used to cook a lot with my mother and grandmother. It was fabulous! All that feminine energy in the kitchen.

MIA: Now, for real: I *can't* cook.

SAM: Girl, cooking is *social*. Let's hurry up. I'm hungry. Meg, are you ready?

> MIA *exits.* MEG *starts to undress.* SAM *is in total shock.* MEG *covers her mouth, begging her to be silent.* SAM *excuses herself and leaves.*

Scene III

Appendix

Meg takes the robe off completely. We see she has no breasts, but two big scars. The scars attempt to tell a story, but let's face it, they can't do that. It would be too convenient if our bodies could tell what they have endured. What we have made them endure. Vibrant, strong silence should be felt. However, it is not intimidating. It is rather meant to crush the social stigmas associated with a "certain fixed embodiment." In the background, juxtaposed, projections of Alexandros of Antioch's "Aphrodite of Milos" and Michelangelo Buonarrotti's "David." Meg puts the robe back while looking with mixed reactions at the two sculptures. She says the monologue while pacing. Every now and then, she stops, but resumes pacing almost immediately. Mid-speech, Mia wants to enter, but remains caught in the liminal space of that door. She listens carefully and is in total shock. She did not know about her sister's gut-wrenching "story" and their grandma's cause of death. She is overwhelmed. She cries. Sam holds her. Both women stay outside of the stage. Except for Meg, the audience should be able to see them.

MEG: When I was younger, I used to lose my pencils a lot. I left home with three and returned with one, *if* lucky. My mother didn't know, so I used my own savings to buy pencils and when I ran out of money, I just begged my classmates to lend me one. One time, I came back home without my entire backpack. My mother was furious, "How did you not notice? Didn't it feel different?" I raised my shoulders and hesitated to answer, and she got even angrier. She said, "In life, ..." Come on, like you need me to tell you anything that starts like that. No one does. Life comes in waves, sometimes we like their gentle caress, other times they're so violent, like a slap. Life offers us a lot of pain and sorrow. But we have to march on. There is no other solution to the bad and the surreal in our lives. Like one time, I was so ready to start my job, I had all the qualifications, and then I was told, "Look, dear, we are sorry, but after careful consideration, we chose to offer it to a different one." You know that person is not even half as good as you are, but you can't change anything. Or, listen to this one. You are on vacation, it's summer, it's beautiful, you enjoy your cocktail on the boardwalk, when all of a sudden you hear people screaming and that noise becomes louder and louder, and you have no freaking clue what's going on until the crowd takes you with them and then, from a protective place, you see how a disturbed criminal rams into innocent people with his truck and you pinch yourself in disbelief, but you smell the blood of the dead in the air and you realize that this is not a horrible movie. Life, ha, right? (*Pause*) And... these? (*Points to the scars, but does not finish her thought*) When I was in college, I befriended Carmen, who told me, "Meg, in Latin my name behaves like a masculine and a feminine noun, in equal amounts: it's a neuter. 50-50, a perfect balance, something that you can't find in life without passing judgments. It means song or poem, but there is nothing lyrical or soothing in my life. I was born intersex. And for years I managed to hide my truth until I grew up and I couldn't ignore my body's needs. I discovered its *pleasures*. I dissolved my worries and obsessions in the other's body because that's how *liquid* our meat becomes when we make love. But this good feeling was always short-lived. I was called names, horrible names, as if I chose this reality, this embodiment. Meg, do you know how many people are born intersex? 1 in every 100 people! Not many, but instead of being treated with love and respect, we are considered an abject anomaly. I look at my body many times. I do not see *anything* abnormal. It's quite complex and interesting. I have been told that I had to choose. But how would I know if I am a man or a woman? What if I choose and then regret my choice? Why can't I be *both*?" That night I made love with Carmen and it was the *best* thing I have ever experienced. I wanted to run away with Carmen, if... (*wipes her tears*). *Fuck* these tears! *Fuck* haters! I went to Carmen's apartment. I had a spare key. I opened the door. It smelled divine, of lavender. I have always wanted to make love in a lavender field. I called, "Carmen, Carmen." No answer. And then I saw Carmen, on the floor. The mirror, Carmen's silent therapist during all those years, was shattered all over Carmen's body. Its huge wooden frame stayed intact. Carmen looked like a painting. So serene. But Carmen was dead. *We* push people away and make them feel like they amount to nothing. After Mia's cancer and her obsessive desire to become a mother, I had an epiphany: I was looking at her pain, ingesting her addition of torture, I was noticing how she took out her breast after a *long* introspection, and then I did the BRCA test. It turned out I inherited the faulty gene, too, fucking great, right? and would develop cancer. So, I said to myself: why the fuck should I wait for cancer to pay me a visit when I can be a *previvor*? I *am* a lawyer; I know my rights! I made the decision to have a preventive surgery. No doctor could tell me otherwise. I was crying tears not because of my decision, but because I was thinking of Carmen. I am still a woman even without breasts. (*Beat*) My little sister... (*sighs*) ... she has a fucked up masochistic way to manage pain. (*Sarcastic*) Thanks, mom, for not telling us about cancer. The sickening secrecy! Now I know how grandma died. So what?! It's too fucking late!

> MEG *starts walking toward the screens; takes a bat and smashes the sculptures of "Aphrodite of Milos" and "David." Obviously, this is a symbolic gesture. End this scene with images of women who had mastectomy and are proud "flat sisters."* SAM *and* MIA *join* MEG *on stage. They hold one another. After a few moments,* MEG *leaves with* SAM.

<u>Scene 3</u>

In the living room, there is a huge poster with Mia naked and another with Betty Boop. On the couch the dress is still not finished. Mia stands in front of the posters evaluating them. The best way to describe Mia's is to make a social commentary on Betty Boop's. Mia's is neither innocent, nor vulgar. As shown in the poster, Mia has finally taken her robe off, exposed and accepted her scar, which now reads "Dignity" (i.e., the tattoo). When the scene begins, Mia does not face the audience. Mia listens to Beyoncé's "If I were a boy" and sings: "... It's a little too late for you to come back, Say, it's just a mistake, Think I'd forgive you like that..."

MARK: No more Hopper. (*Claps*)

MIA: Jesus, you scared me!

MARK: Sorry, I didn't mean to. What are you writing?

MIA (*Reads what's written on the poster*): "This is a <u>real</u> woman with one breast and one Dignity."

> MARK *scratches his head.*

MIA: We need to *record* our pain, just as we keep track of our birthdays, weddings, and holidays. Pain plays an equal part in our identity.

MARK (*Distracted*): I got my license back today.

MIA: Keep your promise.

MARK: And take you out for a ride?

MIA: No! Tell me why you couldn't drive.

MARK: I'd rather go jogging.

MIA: No *fucking* way! You owe me that story. (*Looks at the poster with herself and taps it*): *We* want to hear it.

MARK: Why do people always want to hear the truth? What's in the past should stay in the past.

MIA: My past misses a piece, and that's your *story.* I heard many horrible medical news and predictions that I've gained immunity. Besides, it's *not* a matter of getting hurt, as it's witnessing your accepting responsibility for whatever stupid thing you did that night.

MARK [This is the beginning of the end]: Brace yourself. (*More to himself*): Oh, boy, boy, oh, *boy*, this shit is gonna be tough. Oh, boy... boy, boy...

MIA (*Exasperated*): *Fuck*, be a man!

MARK (*Speaks holding her shoulders and staring into her eyes*): That night I drank too much. You called and announced that your pregnancy test was positive.

MIA (*Releases herself from his grip*): But ten minutes later I called you again only to be redirected to your answering machine. The second and third pregnancy tests came negative.

MARK: Well, that does not help *now*. When you called, I was afraid. I ended up with a ... (*Stops. Admission of guilt is not in his nature*): ... hooker.

MIA: *I* know. She called here. You left your driver's license at her place.

MARK: You knew?!

MIA: I *did* send your clothes to be cleaned, didn't I?

MARK: It was only *that* time. I swear. I had a one-night stand to prove myself that I was still a free man. (*Takes a step backward*) I didn't want the baby. A few months ago, I had a vasectomy. I wanted to suffer.

MIA: From a vasectomy?! That's practically painless.

MARK (*Ignores her question*): To forget the deep shit we're in, I've started running immediately after the car accident and my one-night stand. I can't tell you this experience didn't mean anything to me.

MIA (*Cynical*): Eye-opening.

MARK: It meant freedom from fatherhood, you, and monogamy.

MIA: Man's most terrifying *domestic* trifecta.

MARK (*Agitated*): Then the *guilt* dumped a load on me. I felt so sorry. The guilt gored me.

MIA (*Very mean*): Poor *baby*, do you need a tampon?

MARK: Arhhhh!

> *She exits; soft music is heard; he starts dancing with MIA's poster.*

MARK (*To the poster*): What I did was horrible. Let's end this dreadful phase in our lives!

MIA (*Reenters; dials a telephone number*): Hi, I'd like to borrow one of your escorts. What type? (*Evaluating him*) Hm, let me think... (*Hesitant at first, then increasing her speed*): Blonde, brunette, red; short, tall; fat, thin; young, ... My cheating husband *is* not picky.

> MARK *grabs the phone. She exits.* MIA *reenters with a webcaster gun and catches him in a spider web.* MARK *does not do anything. He's covered in that sticky mess.* MIA *storms out. Offstage, we hear her:* 'Shower, now! NOOOOOOOOW!"

Scene 4

It's evening. We've moved into summer. We hear Philip Glass' "Metamorphosis." There is no one on stage for a few minutes. Meg enters first; sits down. Then, Mia; sits down. Mark follows her; sits down. Music stops. Silence. Don't rush into dialogue.

MIA (*Matter-of-fact*): I don't understand why you want me to repeat.

MARK: Because I do.

MIA: I leave you. Is it *clear* now?

MARK: Why?

MIA: My loan was approved.

MARK: A loan for what?!

MIA: For a small business with Meg. We'll open a library-café, *Sisterhood*, with burgundy walls, mahogany, vintage-style furniture, transparent, eggshell window covers. Our signature non-alcoholic drink will be *socata*, what our grandma used to make when we were kids. It's a refreshing, lemony beverage.

MARK: Fuck, I know what *socata* is. I drank plenty when we were dating.

MIA: Yeah, I forgot. Sometimes, this (*pointing to the two of them*) feels like a dream.

MARK: Whatever. (*Beat*) Is this your new thing?

MIA: What?

MARK: Opening new businesses. Doing things (*a little bit hesitantly*) behind my back.

MIA: Hypocrite!

MARK: I'm serious.

MIA (*Matter-of-fact*): We'll serve lots of sweet treats. We'll have a good selection of wine. We'll decorate the walls with black-and-white photos from our childhood, and not those standard, cheap photos that one sees in restaurants and hotels. Ah, ... and one big photo with grandma. (*Contemplating*): Maybe one with myself naked? (*Reminiscing a thought, she smiles*): Although Meg wanted to decorate the walls with photos of cats...or of us as cats.

MARK: Is this revenge?

MIA: No, Mark, it's not. When I found out about your whoring around session, I was so devastated. I looked at my body and scolded it: Why, *why* are you so repugnant? Why did you make my husband cheat?

MARK: I am sorry.

MIA: Sorry means nothing to me. For days, I could not sleep, I looked at my scar, at photos with myself young, at these two posters... I could not eat. I felt like shit, but acted like a lady.

    MARK *wants to touch her.*

MIA: *No!* I moved on. I leave you, and that's *final.*

MARK: So, it *is* revenge.

MIA: I don't understand why you're so surprised. When you weren't working late at the bank, you were outside celebrating some minor transactions with your economists.

MARK: I've always invited you out.

MIA: When we were first dating, there was only you and me—a couple. Once we got married, you've added friends to keep *us* company. That's so lame.

MARK: How so?

MIA: I believe that's when one uses friends as an excuse for a fucked-up marriage. Actually, you know what? Even on *our* honeymoon, you invited your best friend, his girlfriend, his sister, your cousin, and your cousin's best friend. That wasn't intimate or celebratory at all! (*Beat*) If only we had an *orgy*... You've added yet another escape from us through jogging. I was practically outside of your life! You came home for food and sex, which lately you've needed less and less.

MARK (*Justifying himself*): I asked those friends to join us on our honeymoon because I am a popular guy who likes to celebrate with as many people as possible. I've started jogging to erase the memory of a one-night stand and to put myself back in shape. I wanted food, but you were bored cooking the two recipes you knew, and never tried new ones. (*Desperately,*): I *wanted* sex, but you rejected me, as if I had some contagious condition.

MIA: *Qui s'excuse, s'accuse...*

MARK: Fuck, I've also suffered!

MIA: Suffered, schmuffered... You know what's your problem?

MARK (*Impertinent*): By all means, professor, please share your wisdom.

MIA: I could start with that, but never mind... Your problem is that you don't know how to *feel* a woman. It's not entirely your fault, though; you come from a long misogynistic lineage. Like grandfather, like father, like son. Your mother earned her bachelor's degree *magna cum laude*, but ended up doing laundry, cooking, mopping floors, bit by bit erasing the memory of having once been an aspiring intellectual.

MARK: Leave *my* mother alone. She never complained.

MIA (*Sarcastic*): *Shocking*! And who in your family would've given a rat's ass?! When you had that car accident and slept with that stranger, you were scared that you *might* become a father. You used that *woman's body*. You never knew how to speak with women. Well, I'm done *interpreting* what women say.

MARK: That woman is a sex worker.

MIA: Go fuck yourself!

MARK [I can't believe this shit is happening] (*Scared*): Mia, sweetie, can I start working with you? (*With emphasis*): For you?

MIA: Wanna be my whore?

MARK: What?!

MIA: Meg and I will open that library-café for *fun*. We've decided that we wasted half of our lives trying to establish who we are so we don't mess up our limiting, archaic, good for recycling, fucked up system.

MARK (*Stammering*): What...am I supposed... to do... without you?

    MIA *raises her shoulders with cold indifference.*

MARK: You've been like a... like a... (*finding his courage,*) you've been *mothering* me (*tries to be cute*), baby.

MIA: Guilty as charged!

MARK: I can't live without you. I beg you to stay. (*No response. Commands her with no conviction*): I order you to stay! (*Gets back to a friendly tone*): Come on, let's discuss more. I could come up with some ideas for your restaurant, get you a better loan...

MIA: For the *millionth* time, it's a library-café, and you're not part of it! Look (*checks the time on her wristwatch to avoid eye contact*), it's getting late.

MARK: You're right. Let's go to bed.

MIA: It's *over.*

MARK: You *can't* end a relationship by yourself. We got married together, *we* should end it together.

MIA: Was it fair when only you had an affair?

MARK (*Unmasked stupidity*): I had *courage* to do what I did. I thought it would be refreshing and would motivate us to start anew.

MIA: What are we? A car that needs a new battery?! Men and their superhero obsession. I bet when you were *cumming,* you must have had this perfect image of Asclepius holding his staff and miraculously healing our marriage.

MARK: *Stop*!

MIA goes out for a second and brings a small box.

MIA: I bought you a hermit crab. Make sure you buy a new shell when it outgrows it. That's how they get rid of what it's too small and not working anymore. (*Pause*) One more thing. I called Doctor Lorne.

MARK: Doctor who?

MIA: Oops, sorry, Doctor-*Pussy*. I told him you'd like your vasectomy reversed.

MARK is speechless.

MEG: The cab is downstairs.

MIA: Perfect timing. (*To* MARK): Take care of the hermit crab!

MIA and MEG leave.

MARK (*Calls* PETE): Oh my God, man, you aren't gonna fucking believe what just happened to me... Mia left. Yes, she did. Can you believe that?... What?! You *can*??? (*Pause*) Why didn't *you* warn me? What?! You couldn't interfere? *Fuck* you! (*Beat*) Could I come over? No, it's not a good time? (*Hurt*) Some friend. God! (*Beat*)

He hangs up. Moves around aimlessly; finds a note.

MARK: "Our bedroom is <u>empty</u>. You're welcome."

MIA's decision starts to sink in.

MARK: What have *I* done? (*Louder*) What the fuck have *I*

done??? Shit! I need my sneakers to run. *Now!* (*Starts looking for them. Exasperated,*): God, I can't find anything by myself.

> *He starts throwing a pair of boots, a bag, a medical robe, a regular robe, a kimono, gauze, cotton balls, a doll,* MIA's *still unfinished self-designed dress, bras, a brown paper bag full with pink ribbons which Mark scatters on the floor, a sexy lingerie in an unopened box, a jar of gummy bears, and a replica of a prototype for a "gummy bear" breast implant. Stops. Opens the jar of gummy bears. Chews loudly. Looks at the lingerie. Looks at the prototype for the breast implant and plays with it. Startled, he thinks he has heard something.*

MARK: Mia? Is that you, sweetie? I knew you couldn't leave *me.*

> *No response. He notices the poster with* MIA. *He touches it. From that pile he takes out the kimono that he wore in the previous scene. Puts it on. Gets frustrated. Takes the kimono off. Rips it. Goes back to the poster. Wants to rip that, too. On the back he discovers an inscription: "To my <u>mark</u>, goodbye." He throws the poster on the ground and stomps on it with anger. At one point, a chair falls and then another.* MARK *lifts them up. As he does that, he realizes the hermit crab has left behind its shell.*

MARK (*Holding the empty shell,*): Fuck, where is this damn crab?!

> *To suggest* MARK's *maddening state of mind, we hear a series of different styles of music, which are interrupted abruptly (i.e., we hear a song for a few fleeting seconds), thus creating a necessary cacophony, as if someone is constantly changing radio stations, like a misplaced, yet mischievous Deus ex machina. Since it has lost its erstwhile capacity to fix humans' entangled problems, this mysterious force finds itself spreading even more*

chaos than there is. Overwhelmed, MARK *runs away. Lights stay on as if expecting* MARK *or* MIA *to return. That does not happen. Instead, a noise is finally heard, most likely made by the hermit crab. We see the crab walking on the poster with* MIA. *This should be done via a projection or a prop. This is all that is left of this couple, and, ironically, this is an intruder, an outsider, a third party, or a very bitter "side-effect" of the dis-ease.*

END OF PLAY

Endnotes:
1. Deep Brain Stimulation: This play's first version was written in 2011. Since then, many discoveries should have occurred.
2. Blessing the walls: Meg refers to a ritual that is still performed in some Christian Orthodox countries. However, a priest should be doing it to secure its sacred nature.

Post-Scriptum:

Mental and emotional response to breast cancer has been a topic discussed at length. My approach is from two angles; one is emotional resilience and the other one is movement. Breast cancer like any other type of cancer is a traumatic experience. Humans are naturally equipped with the right amount of resilience to survive. When we experience trauma, the internal protective system is under threat. One of the consequences of this threat is lowering emotional resilience. As a therapist, I encourage the use of the body as a vehicle for self-awareness, expression, and healing. When we increase self-awareness by tuning into the body's sensations and emotions, we also increase our emotional resilience. The area(s) affected by cancer may be sensed physiologically and mentally as numb. Numbness translates in the human's mind as powerlessness. The rest of the body is not deprived of the power of sensation. Through movement, we experience a sense of integration of all parts of the body regardless of the sensation of numbness. A movement practiced with application in cancer treatment is allowing the body and mind to experience contrasts. The movement of opposite sensations and emotions creates new reference points. One part of the body is affected by the illness, another one is not. One part of the body is numb, another one is not. The awareness of opposites' existence in the physical, emotional, and mental body increases the overall resilience. Another benefit of practicing the movement of opposite sensations is the increase of boundary knowledge. Why is that important? Being aware of internal boundaries is like a lantern in the dark. When a body part suffers from an illness, all the other parts step in to give support. Through observation and awareness, the human system, as intelligent as it is, allows body parts to participate in the healing process. The design of each part's role is set on by healthy internal boundaries. In movement, practice questions like "Where in my body do I experience aliveness?" or "Did I notice any shift in my body from pain to relief?" are vehicles to increase body awareness.

In her play *Mia*, Catalina Florescu touches the nerve of pain, suffering, and conformity through the mélange of resilience and escape.

Meg takes the robe off. We see she has no breasts, but two big scars. The scars attempt to tell a story, but let's face it, they can't do that. It would be too convenient if our bodies could tell what they have endured. What we have made them endure. Vibrant, strong silence should be felt. However, it is not intimidating. It is rather meant to crush the social stigmas associated with a "certain fixed embodiment."

The emotional resilience is intoxicating. It's born from the uncomfortable, from checking-in with reality with boldness. The escape is a cathartic movement, a redirection, a reset despite the fear and resentment.

In the therapy experience, the physiological cure is not guaranteed, but the choices in the treatment process are real. Body awareness increases emotional resilience, while theater, art, movement are choices. As Viktor Frankel so eloquently said, our power of choosing shapes our growth and freedom – **Mihaela Campion**, Licensed Clinical Psychotherapist

I am a person who likes to be provoked, contradicted, questioned, etc. The content of Catalina's work always does exactly that, which is very exciting and fulfilling as an artist. In the process of working on Mark in *Mia* I discovered he is an archetype rather than a stereotype in our society. This is always a great playground for me to have been provided a platform to find a way and make alive something opposite of what I am as a person, the norms, beliefs, viewpoints, ethics of mine, etc. In this thought and mind provoking process you grow as an artist and a human being. The bigger the questions posed, the deeper you dive into unknown waters. In that archeological like seemingly everlasting process of never knowing when and what you are going to discover, you reveal much of who you really are. It is always a self-discovery process and through that in detail detection of new angles, layers and aspects of yourself you bring a new dimension in your craft and to the character you are painting at the given moment. This makes you reevaluate yourself who you are; what you are; where you are and why you are in the now, on the way to the everlasting journey of shaping yourself, or as Tarkovsky would say "sculpting in time." The physical aspect of the character of Mark was totally me, but the emotional and the viewpoint aspect is opposite me: Where do these two opposites collide, where do they meet, where is the challenge of it, the balance of it, how do I find the truth and justify it, good, bad, or ugly, to ultimately embody and illuminate the character with no judgment, unconditionally in a vibrant, alive and multilayered spectrum of life that would be a magnet to the individual in the society and an example to study, explore, reference, and investigate – **Tony Naumovski**, actor

SNOWDROPS AND CHLORINE

SNOWDROPS AND CHLORINE

The play brings into question the urgency to invalidate breast cancer as an illness diagnosed exclusively to women, and instead to expand our knowledge to accommodate men and trans as part of this dialogue.

Script history

Developed with the support from AFCN (the Romanian National Cultural Fund Association), the play was supposed to premiere in Bucharest in 2020. Due to C-19, however, the play was adapted to fit the restrictions of this new medium, Zoom "Theatre." Not only that, but I was also working against an invisible, yet stressful "clock," since the funds had to be used during a specific period of time (otherwise, they would have been lost). I had the extreme luck to work with Reg Flowers who was familiar with *Mia* when we taught it together during our honors course "21st century Dramatic Texts." They are also an expert in the Theater of the Oppressed, which was a wonderful bonus.

It is my strong belief that we shush our bodies and minds, thus becoming our greatest oppressors. Through this play, and the series by extension, my effort and ambition are to expose some of the reasons why we do that. Of the three in the trilogy, *Snowdrops and Chlorine* is the most technical of all. The play premiered on August 5th, 2020 on the YouTube Channel of Falconworks Theatre Company, where it can still be viewed for free. Please be advised that the play in this volume ends differently than its recorded version. Compare and contrast, and give feedback.

Post Zoom Premiere -- A Few Thoughts

Snowdrops and Chlorine has holes. Some were made because at the moment Zoom "Theater" does not allow actors and actresses to use their bodies fully. Most certainly Zoom "Theater" carries the imperfections of technology. We can click on this and that, but it's not even remotely close to the *feel* of a stage, to movement, to looking into a thespian's eyes, and to clap when actors take a bow. Zoom "Theater" is also a cheating experience. If we are honest, we will "watch" and/or "do" at least two things simultaneously, making that online theatrical moment a screen-in-a-screen, spiritually depleted experience. Pre-C-19, this is how we operated online. The temptation is too strong, and we have not (yet) learned how to discipline our minds, how to quiet them so we enjoy one virtual play at a time and *nothing* else. We would not be in two theaters simultaneously, would we?!

Snowdrops and Chlorine has holes in the script, too. I chose to write it like this because I was imagining characters meeting in oncology wards, nodding politely or wearily, starting a conversation, or barely making any sounds, wanting to get the hell out of that smell, that artificial light, that reminder of their bodies being broken. I wanted to write a piece where we meet characters more than in "medias res," who are still haunted by their cancer experience, from their diagnosis to treatments to cost to lack of support. When GABBY asks TEDDY, "what is a hospital?", that is a literal translation of a legal definition that exists in Romania. When TEDDY talks about greedy managers, that's a fact. In Romania, there is a crisis at the level of finding treatments and the painful reminder that the system works *if* you know someone who knows someone else who ..., you get my point. When I write about elephants almost never getting cancer, that is a fact. When I talk about these random cancerous mutations, that is also a fact. When A HUSBAND is desperate and recounts his story, the oncotype DX is not fictional. When GABBY goes to have a preventive double mastectomy, she speaks about genetic tests and their result *prior* to being diagnosed. When she talks about "wolves," that is a moment I witnessed when my own mother was dying and delirious. All these are *intentional* holes in a traditional plot because I did not care about an arc, about character development, about climax, about pity and terror. Instead, I wanted to examine a body broken, a couple broken, and a family broken, and do that *microscopically* because cancer hurts a lot!

In the script, *Snowdrops and Chlorine* ends with the public coming on stage to hit a piñata designed by Thedra Cullar-Ledford, a breast cancer survivor. In Zoom "Theater," we couldn't do that. I'm positive that hitting a piñata collectively would bring closure. Because a play must end. Finally, Dan Basu joined our team and, via his live artwork, made Zoom "Theater" feel a little bit less technical and alienating.

Industry praises

Playwright Catalina Florescu's *Snowdrops and Chlorine* is a clarion cry for women's health and reproductive justice in not only her home country, but also globally. Writing this piece was pushed forward in activism from the playwright's own experience in caring for her mother during her brave battle with a particularly aggressive breast cancer. From this real-life testimony, she has literally taken the care-giving experience and turned it into a radical exploration into the fault lines in the treatment of suffering patients, and the dirty politics of public health. In short, Catalina has transformed her shared stories and grief into art.

As an actress, I was humbled by the rehearsal and performance process for the virtual presentation. As a woman of color who has watched breast, ovarian, and cervical cancers consume my community and family, I was immediately touched by the universality of the piece. The play targets specific health information (including men's breast cancer) without sounding preachy or feeling like an evening of *agit-prop*.

The incredible use of the melding of past and present timeline presents actors with the wonderful challenge of embodying the same characters at different ages and circumstances. While the plotline and narrative are linear, the destabilizing effect of playing with the construct of *time* itself, centers an emotional landscape that, like cancer, one never knows what every new minute, hour, day will bring. During this current era of the COVID-19 pandemic, we are reminded daily about the fragility of life, and this play is particularly resonant, and rich.

Not only does it provide actors the opportunity to explore the full range of emotion, conflict, recollection, relationships, and grace, but it also expertly drops gems of information and data. Just as Larry Kramer's *The Normal Heart* is more than an "a play about AIDS," *Snowdrops & Chlorine* is so much more than just "a play about breast cancer." I know that a major component of Catalina's mission is to have the play serve as a gathering space and gateway for panelists, experts, and survivors to share their experiences. That the vision for this piece extends beyond the play into discourse, discussion, and shared fellowship, is a heartening reminder about the healing power of the arts – **Caroline Stefanie Clay**, actress, Assistant Professor, Iowa University

As a cancer survivor, in my case I was given a 50% chance of surviving the year after diagnosis, and so, revisiting those feelings was not an easy choice. However, I am glad I did. With *Snowdrops and Chlorine*, thanks to Catalina's kind guidance and the supportive atmosphere she created, the experience for me destigmatized my own feelings on the subject, and hopefully did the same for those who participated in the performance – **Christopher Bailey**, The World Health Organization's Arts and Health Lead

When I was presented with the opportunity to be part of *Snowdrops and Chlorine*, I jumped into it because it sounded so interesting. The story is unique. I had no idea that men can have breast cancer. I had to do extensive research to get an understanding of this to approach the character realistically and sincerely, yet making it my own. The script provided a lot of details which made it easier to understand and have sympathy and hope for the character(s). The age range of my male character was older than what I usually get cast in, but I love a challenge because I knew it would be a great experience and it would enhance my craft.

The idea of doing a virtual event didn't phase me one bit. I'm extremely comfortable using Zoom. It was interesting navigating the entrances and exits of the character, enhancing my movement within a frame, and of course, making sure all the technical stuff on my end was on point. For me, a virtual theatrical event is like doing a film. One must work within the frame and really take advantage of the camera with all the tricks you can do as an actor. I'm grateful for this opportunity because I learned a lot about breast cancer. I have more awareness, respect, and hope for breast cancer patients and survivors – **Khalid Rivera**, actor and singer

I was approached by Catalina Florescu to be part of this play she wrote as a survivor of male breast cancer and to help with questions and answers after the play's debut. This play is part of her series on staging breast cancer. As a more than a decade male breast cancer survivor, I was honored to take part and share my story with the cast. Everyone was so professional in their craft I felt a little out of place, as I had no experience in this arena. Watching the director bring the characters to life was truly something to observe.

In this play, Catalina brings to light that breast cancer is a people's disease, and not gender specific. As a man surviving this disease, I can really appreciate her take on how the character Teddy went through so many emotions, even contemplating suicide. So many men are embarrassed to talk about this disease, and I can see how someone might go down that dark path. Having writers like Catalina bring a male character into this play helps enlighten theatergoers that male breast cancer is a *real* disease and much more needs to be researched. 2,620 men will be diagnosed this year alone (2020, A.N.) in the United States and unfortunately 520 of them will die due to the later stages of their diagnosis. This is due to men not being educated about the early warning signs as women are, and also being embarrassed to talk about their breasts until it's too late.

Thank you, Catalina, for helping shed an important light through your writing – **Michael Singer**, male breast cancer survivor

Characters:
GABBY, 45-50, lawyer
TEDDY, 30-35, former fitness instructor, former sprint champion
AN ANATOMY TEACHER/A HUSBAND/A FATHER/A CIVILIAN, early 30's
"ELEONOR" (Ideally played by a breast cancer survivor)
Please read the appendix.

Absentees:
A HUSBAND'S WIFE
GABBY'S SISTER
A FATHER'S DAUGHTER

*Please **make** the absentees' presence **feel** as if they are with us. Interrupt the script/play by listening to a song, or by observing a minute of silence, or by laughing. We can't program our emotions, but we should remind ourselves of the others' energies that we have been deprived of prematurely. If the Furies are known as the chthonic goddesses of vengeance, what if we come up with something that could help us soothe our open wounds? We are one person less with one whom we lost, yet ironically, we weigh more because they are inside of us. The frustration comes when we can't touch them, or cry and laugh with them, etc. The trauma returns when we see the greediness of any medical system, to say the least.*

Time:
Present day, some flashbacks.

Place:
Various spaces.

Special note:

In a patriarchal and misogynistic country such as Romania, my ambition was to develop a male character diagnosed with this illness. Through him, I teach several lessons. One of them is that this is not an illness diagnosed exclusively to women. Second, no one in Teddy's family had breast cancer, so his case illustrates that not all cancers are hereditary, another myth that needs to be destroyed. Finally, Teddy has zero support from his father, whom he wants to impress and who, in return, always puts Teddy down. Teddy is *attacked* not only by his body, but also by his father's ignorance or, worse, misinformation.

Sadly, Romania is not an isolated case. I mention it because, in part, the research for this play comes from data from that country. Still, cancer attacks beyond borders! So, if people begin to understand the tragedy that happens with this character, <u>maybe</u> they would treat breasts with maturity and respect, rather than obsessively perceive them through sexual lenses and/or reductively through lactating stages. Ultimately, my goal with this trilogy is to fight for implementing a mandatory screening program, as well as to expose the utter futility of products designed to raise "awareness" for breast cancer.

<u>Note for directors and readers</u>:

When discussing the script and its transition to stage, please consider Bertolt Brecht heavily. Also keep in mind that I do not want to break the fourth wall per se, as I prefer to use my energy to build new spaces where we all feel comfortable to undress and talk about our bodies. All scenes are announced via written titles on a cardboard box that will subtly transition to words written on various parts of the protagonists' bodies.

Everything that is written in bold is pre-taped and shown as a movie (clip). The play is metatheatrical and multi-media. More, these bold (sic!) parts all show the moment when each character was told the diagnosis, as well as when one character met with a bereaving father. Since the readers and/or the audience must experience these fragments differently, the goal here is to clearly delineate this transformation from a person with a social status to a patient who may begin his/her/their isolation behind closed doors. But <u>what if</u> we stop ignoring their cries and *open* these hospital walls? Like schools and prisons, hospitals are enclosed spaces. We must discontinue this oppressive, selfish practice. Furthermore, these parts typed in bold are a flashback, and they allow each character to confront his/her/their own past, to view it with detachment, and to have a disembodied yet learning experience. No one teaches us how to react, and so, sometimes, we are lost, angry, confused. But <u>what if</u> we knew how *to start* how to react, <u>what if</u> we knew how *to rehearse* **that** beginning? Create some lines. Play with them. Reflect.

Prologue

The scene appears empty. One by one, each character is in the spotlight. One chair is empty. The setting is split into four equal parts, which have continuity (and may resemble the four chambers of the human heart). Like before, these parts are presented one by one: a long row of hospital beds + neon lights + linoleum; a long row of school desks + neon lights + linoleum; a Courthouse; and a park. The spotlight makes one more round, this time directed at the audience. It feels like a Morse code only that with lights. The spotlight stops. We are in a hospital, which is announced in a Brecht-like style. After that, we transition into a cinematic moment with Teddy recounting his transformation from a person into a patient, or the shock of hearing the news.

TEDDY: **The first time when they told me I had cancer I looked in a mirror and, like a "real" man, full with testosterone, I smashed it into pieces. Thank God I was already in a hospital, they cleaned that wound, put gauze, and told me to go to a pharmacy and take a sedative. They told me to calm down, drink tea... I was enraged. "Cancer? Breast cancer???" Tell me, when was the last time when you saw a reasonable person breaking a mirror? I was feeling like a criminal whom I ... I stole his body. My *own* body... I had to keep quiet because all around me I was hearing, "It will go away... It will go away..." And just when I thought it was over and I could go out, I heard a nurse asking: "Do you believe in God?" I shook my head. She went on, "Dear, go to a church... start praying... you know... so you will be healed." Honestly, I wanted to break another mirror, but I knew that if I did that they would consider me a raving lunatic and lock me some place... *safe*. I felt like I couldn't breathe, so I stormed out of that place..."**

A loud sound is followed by a montage of "natural" disasters.

Scene One

The International Women's Day

TEDDY (*Running,*): Let this end. Let today be the last day. No, not the last day of my life, come on, ... Just the last day when I come to this hospital.

> TEDDY *stops running. He goes to a stack of magazines and brochures walled on one side of* **The Waiting Room**. *He seems to be searching for something, but it's not clear what. He finally picks up a magazine.*

TEDDY (*Ironic*): "Ten easy exercises to be fit and healthy. (*Throws the magazine towards a poster adjacent to the stack of magazines. That poster reads,* "MENS SANA IN CORPORE SANO") Mens sana, my ass! I *was* a junior sprint champion. I came home with gold medals. I *had* dreams...

> TEDDY *starts to walk faster. He takes his jacket off and checks his phone.*

TEDDY: Where is the nurse? Hello???

> TEDDY *resumes walking. Starts to laugh.*

TEDDY: I can't believe this! (*Points to the phone*): This douchebag got married??? All he cared for was to eat and sleep, eat and sleep...

> TEDDY *becomes increasingly aware of his body. He tries to cover himself, to make himself invisible. His hands are on his chest. Then, he is even more agitated. He stands up and does some pushups. He drinks water without stopping. He then takes a jump rope out of his pocket*

and starts jumping. He counts: 1, 2, 3... All of a sudden, GABBY enters. She is extremely sexy and carries a carry-on bag. She is assertive and funny.

GABBY: Take it easy, dear... The whole building is shaking. You know it's about to collapse.

TEDDY: Collapse?!

GABBY: They should have destroyed it after the last earthquake...

She gives him a hug.

TEDDY (*Realizing she came with a carry-on bag,*): Where are you going?

GABBY (*Smiles*): To a VIP teambuilding. (*Vaguely*): You know ... the case...

TEDDY: Hmm... but what I told you, ... stays anonymous? I don't want reporters to follow me around...

GABBY(*Subtle*): But, sweetie, you have immunity...

TEDDY: The hell I do...

GABBY: Did you talk to your father? Did you convince him to help you?

TEDDY: He is ... (*Sad*) He said, "Stop checking yourself in a mirror. Be a man!"

GABBY: One day you should introduce him to me... I'd kick his ass.

TEDDY: He is strong like a mammoth.

GABBY: Those are extinct.

TEDDY: You are the only one who saw me naked. (*Points to the pectoral area*)

GABBY: You worry about that, while others make a fortune out of our misery...

TEDDY: What are you even talking about?

GABBY (*Taps on her carry-on bag*): This one... this case ... about a doctor who misinformed her patients ... who died.

TEDDY: Be careful.

GABBY: Careful??? My dear, *we* are breast cancer survivors waiting for a nurse to check on us in a very old building about to collapse. I am not afraid!

> *The lights go off. What we see projected is a black and white movie shot in the fashion of very old movies, meaning, it is interrupted by cuts. Those cuts, however, are a very subtle way to introduce the mastectomy procedure to the public. The spotlight returns to illuminate the poster MENS SANA IN CORPORE SANO and another one, CANCER IS CURED WITH A SMILE. Now we see the two of them engaged in practicing how to "win" cancer with a smile. Their faces are like masks. Lights are back on.*

GABBY (*Mix of feelings*): Teddy, keep doing that. Don't give up. Smile. See? Cancer is ... gone.

TEDDY: Laughter does cure everything.

GABBY: That and (*sniffs*) chlorine.

TEDDY: I wash my clothes twice after each hospital visit.

GABBY: Really? (*Sniffs her blouse. Excited,*): This is the smell of hours of waiting, hoping, crying.... A little bit of menthol, a touch of *fleurs de Provence*, dirty money, and chlorine.

TEDDY: They *invest* in our bodies.

GABBY: Yep, with chlorine. (*Stands up*)" Where is the nurse? (*Calls various names, and then, facing* TEDDY,): Oh, my God! Today is March 8th.

TEDDY: So???

GABBY: Women do not go to work today.

> *They laugh wholeheartedly as if, "Yeah, right, let's see that happening..." They both exit calling various names. Projected, we see Brecht-like signs with the name "snowdrops" written on them. In Romania, these flowers are considered one of "vestitorii primaverii," signaling a new season of rebirth after another long winter.*

Scene Two

Back to School

The previous hospital waiting room "becomes" a classroom. Same neon lights. Same coldness. Same sanitized space. Create a feel of a fossilized atmosphere, i.e., of things stuck in a toxic past. TEDDY *and* GABBY *play new roles, as if they reversed to their teen years, despite the age gap between them.* AN ANATOMY TEACHER *enters.*

AN ANATOMY TEACHER: Good morning!

No one answers.

AN ANATOMY TEACHER: Quiet down! Today is a ... difficult day.

TEDDY: How come?

The teacher sits down. He takes out a jar. Inside of it there is a pair of breasts preserved in formaldehyde, which is, of course, beyond absurd.

GABBY: What is that???

AN ANATOMY TEACHER (*Ignores the question. Lowers a screen. Clears his voice*): Today.... today we learn about the female anatomy.

We hear giggles.

AN ANATOMY TEACHER: Keep joking... do that... No one passes my class!

GABBY: Why?

AN ANATOMY TEACHER (*Clears his voice. Tries to talk. Takes a candy out of his pocket. Unwraps it. Puts it in his month. Takes his time. On a screen we can see schematically the female anatomy. Clears again his voice. Opens his textbook*): Last week we learned about the male anatomy. Just examine this image. (*Complete ignorance*): If you come to think about it, there are few differences. Look!

GABBY: Did you speak with the Religious Studies teacher?

AN ANATOMY TEACHER: About?

GABBY (*Chewing gum even more annoyingly,*): Well, am I *allowed* to speak? (*Makes a chewing gum bubble and pops it immediately*)

AN ANATOMY TEACHER: What did that teacher say?

GABBY (*Plays with the chewing gum through her fingers*): Nothing new... that the woman was made from Adam's rib.

TEDDY: Word.

    GABBY *pinches* TEDDY.

TEDDY: Ouch!

AN ANATOMY TEACHER: Stop crying like a little girl.

GABBY: You are wrong.

AN ANATOMY TEACHER: About...?

GABBY: I read online that pain is pain is pain, regardless of gender.

AN ANATOMY TEACHER (*Rude*): So, you know how to read... Making progress. (*Beat*) How many times do I have to tell you to stop chewing gum during my class? Get up and throw that in the garbage.

GABBY: Fine, fine. But can I say more about pain?

AN ANATOMY TEACHER (*Visibly annoyed*): No! Return to your seat. Now!!!

GABBY (*Confident*): "Pain is ..." (*Makes eye-contact with* TEDDY *who has a sign written on a card box. From the top,*) "Pain is an unpleasant sensory or emotional experience associated with actual or potential tissue damage or described in terms of such damage." (*To the teacher*): It does not say that women should feel more pain than men. (*Picks up the jar and looks at it. Makes a stupefied face*)

AN ANATOMY TEACHER: Give it back!

GABBY: Fine, but what's this???

AN ANATOMY TEACHER: Sit down *now!* (*Returns to the image and points to the breasts*) Let's start with this part. (*Reads*): "In women, breasts have a nipple in the central part surrounded by a pigmented area called the areola. The skin of the areola is slightly deformed by the orifices of the sebaceous glands, sweat glands, and hair follicles." That's it. Open your textbooks, read, then... quiz. (*Keeps the jar in his hands. Now his face is partly hidden*)

GABBY: What, ... when?

AN ANATOMY TEACHER: Today, what do you mean when?

GABBY: Damn!

TEDDY: Shhhh....

GABBY: I left my textbook at home.

    GABBY *raises her hand.*

AN ANATOMY TEACHER: What now?

GABBY: Our school nurse told us to examine our breasts frequently... you know... for *lumps* and stuff. She said it was very important.

AN ANATOMY TEACHER: That's it! Get out! You are suspended for the rest of the day, and you get an F, too.

GABBY (*To the audience, showing how to conduct a self-exam*): Like this. Come on! What's the big deal? What's with this taboo? (*Continues to do her self-exam. Stops and picks up the jar*): Are these boobs?!

AN ANATOMY TEACHER: What, suspension is not enough for you? Do you want to be expelled?

>*She opens the jar.*

GABBY: This stinks!

AN ANATOMY TEACHER: Out!

>*As she walks off stage clearly unfazed by the teacher's threats, we see projected various types of breasts. From that we move to "Freedom" by Yoko Ono.* GABBY *returns, but she is <u>not</u> a teen anymore. She is at her current age. She holds the jar in her hands.*

GABBY: Boobs trapped in a jar! I'd laugh, if this wasn't true! I will never forget that day in school. (*A pause*) We don't live enjoying or knowing our skins. Take me, for example. I lost 40 years thinking that I had to follow what I was told... in schools, from my teachers.... In church, by priests... in bed, by my partners... On TV, from all the ads to products that should make me feel younger, prettier, more desirable... My body is *so* different than what is photoshopped in magazines... My body has wounds. This one is from chickenpox. This one is from when I was pretending I was a gymnast and fell. And these (*points to her breasts*) are from when I had mastectomy.

> *We see projected some clips from "Cancerland" or "Runaway to Recovery." This moment is set against a montage of images of the human body as illustrated schematically in anatomy textbooks, followed by several "must-have" products to enhance women's targeted "femininity."*

GABBY: Why do we learn about pain only when the needle is inside our veins and the bandage is full with blood? (*Points to the teacher, who is frozen, as if he was trapped in a jar*): Teach students something real for *once*. Like, a normal cell divides and copies its DNA to produce two new cells. As scientists have noticed following a mathematical model based on DNA sequencing and epidemiological data, during this otherwise normal process, mistakes occur.

> *The teacher is not visible any longer.*

GABBY: It is believed that these mistakes could have the potential to become cancer mutations. *Two-thirds* of all recorded forms of cancer are such *random* mutations! The other part to complete the whole is related to hereditary factors, poor care for our bodies, and/or exposure to polluted environments and carcinogens.

> *GABBY bumps into a man. There is something about that man that makes her acknowledge his settling into silence. A door is opened. Images of happy couples and families are presented in slow motion. Another door is*

opened. Images of medical tools, machines, and equipment are presented chaotically.

Scene Three

Grief

A HUSBAND *is seated and looks with affection in a photo album. He may or may not be aware of us.*

A HUSBAND: The bitter taste of loneliness... My story? A team of doctors said that my wife should have had an abortion. She was pregnant and her aggressive treatments for cancer would have brought complications to the fetus. They said we were young and had time to have babies. We listened. We agreed. We cried and accepted to go on with the abortion. Then, she started her chemotherapy. She started to lose her hair. She could not walk properly. So, I bought her a cane. She smiled. At first, I did not realize. Then, she said, "Charlie Chaplin." She adored him. When we were in college, we watched all of his movies. She loved that cane and pretended she was Chaplin. Months passed. We thought her agony was about to end soon. We flew to Canada and visited her cousin. She said my wife should not have had chemotherapy. We both laughed. Her cousin was serious. "I don't lie. Did they give you the Oncotype DX test?" We shook our heads. "I called you several times. I even left a message on your answering machine." She called a wrong number. Now that we knew about the test, it was too late... We were *furious*. We came back home. We tried and tried to have a child. It was impossible. My wife was now cancer-free, but could not get pregnant. She should have never had chemo. Why didn't they tell us about Oncotype DX??? Who benefitted from this ... *omission*? Was this a malpractice case? One day, I woke up and found a note and the cane leaning against a wall. Each day, each night, I keep tormenting myself: What the fuck is cancer?!

>A HUSBAND *continues to look through his photo album while projected we read a little bit about this test. Lights off.*

Scene Four

Get Real!

We are inside a Courthouse. This scene <u>appears</u> like a fictionalized litigious case caught during its closing statements. After GABBY *says her brief part, the focus goes to a real breast cancer survivor.*

GABBY: Your Honor, Members of the Jury, Audience, in closing, my client's case must be analyzed professionally, with detachment, so that we have unbiased reactions. My client was not just another medical case. The increased and alarming number registered by the Oncology Department suggests that there should be ways to intervene to request a national screening program to become mandatory for all citizens of our country, regardless of their medical insurance, health status, gender, race, and sex. I lost a dear family member to breast cancer. Our lives are not separated, we live with and through others, and so is a society. A sick person is not a liability. My client could have had a chance. (*Takes out a jar with breasts. Opens it. Shows it to everyone. Pours something that makes the liquid blue. Then puts some things that resemble tumors. Closes the jar. Shakes it vigorously*) When my client called to make an appointment for a mammogram, it should not have been postponed. When she was finally diagnosed, cancer had spread throughout her body. What kind of country is that where there are no national screening programs, where hospitals do not always have treatments, and where we dismiss someone because they are not at "risk"?! What kind of society prefers to wait for a person to get a diagnosis rather than to seek to implement prevention?! This woman had a future. Now, her family has a past. The tragedy of this family could happen to anyone. *When* would we care?!

> *We see images of mammograms and ultrasounds. Then, "ELEONOR," A BREAST CANCER SURVIVOR, enters. She has a short testimony. This should/could vary from representation to representation. While she talks, we see graphic images of cancerous breasts, of scars, etc. This part in the show should be comprised of the author, the director, at least one breast cancer survivor, a family member who has been affected indirectly by the illness, drama therapists, doctors, navigators, nutritionists, pathologists, and the public. This part should be 10 minutes long, or the Romanian equivalent of a break between periods in school. Not all of them will have time to talk. therefore, after each show, there should be a Q & A session.*
>
> *Slowly, the lights are turned off while soft music is played in the background. We see a montage of patients wearing hospital gowns with an emphasis on doors being closed to delineate the social space of the hospital and the intimate space of one's embodiment. When we hear the final door closed, we are "back" in the theater – the mediator between these "worlds."*

Scene Five

Surviving

GABBY *holds a bouquet of snowdrops. She and* TEDDY *are outside and they sit on a bench.*

GABBY: We gotta do something. There are people whose lives were *cut* short. Do you know what's the definition of a hospital?

TEDDY: A place where dreams die.

GABBY: Wrong. "The hospital is a sanitary unit with beds, of public utility, with legal personality, which provides medical services." See, legally, we are covered.

TEDDY: I told you everything I knew.

GABBY: I know, take it easy. I am on your side. But ... those funds.... You know .... They were supposed to reach you ... they were not for pink ribbons and pink banners and pink bracelets...

TEDDY (*Tired*): I KNOW! Look, I can't go on like this... 2 full years. 24 months. 17,520 hours. 1,051,200 minutes. 630,072,000 seconds: cancer-cancer-cancer-cancer-cancer. There must be other words... I can't take it anymore!

GABBY: Teddy, look at me. You are a survivor!

TEDDY: Stop using that word! I am destroyed!

GABBY: Our bodies scar. Underneath our skin there are *land mines* ready to explode at any time.

TEDDY: I did follow all the ads on TV, I ate healthy, I was a national champion in the sprint junior competition. This is *not* my body! I want to break something. (*Looks around. Picks up something and throws that away*) My therapist told me to keep a *gratitude* diary every single day. I said, "What if one day I can't get off of bed, or I vomit, or I crawl on the floor because of the pain, or... what if I feel less than a man?" He said, "Just write..." I did not write one single word.

GABBY (*Matter-of-fact*): Write about the cost of treatment. Write about how you lost your job. Write about how much you hate the word "survivor."

TEDDY: I am a "loser" who *contracted* a "feminine disease." My dad says that repeatedly.

GABBY: When I told my administrative assistant that I had great chances of being diagnosed with breast cancer, she asked if she could be excused. I thought she did not want to look into my eyes. I said, "Fine. Take the day off." After an hour, she came back, handed me a gift bag, and said: "That's all I could find." I had no idea what she meant by that. I opened it and found a book with jokes. She said: "I went to a bookstore, I asked, *What would you recommend for cancer?* and this old gentleman joked, *Votive candles.*" She then looked around and picked up the first book that touched her fingers. You know, randomly. Teddy, cancer is not "feminine," it is not contracted either, it is a *random* mutation in our bodies. These motherfuckers are dormant in our bodies. You are not a "loser," like your father says. Why doesn't he come here, in the hospital? Teddy, *we are alive*!

TEDDY: Alive.. in ... foreign bodies. (*Beat*) Do you go to therapy?

GABBY: I tried.

Darkness.

GABBY: I was in the Courthouse. The phone started to ring. I always turned off my phone at work. Later, when I got home, I noticed there were 7 missed calls. The first one was from a colleague, he wanted to run a case by me, to hear my opinions; another call was from my travel agent, she wanted to tell me about a great deal on Côte d'Azur; a third call was from a neighbor, she was yelling into the phone to boil water when I'd come home since a pipe exploded again... then, I forgot... the last phone: "Good afternoon. We are calling from the lab. We have the results from your BRCA test. Please give us a call when you have a free moment. Thank you, and have a great day!" I called the next day. I could not sleep that night. "Yes, the test results indicate you inherited the faulty gene. Please set up an appointment with your oncologist to review your options." Hm... *Options*?? Fucking great. (*Tries to be funny*): Bring the damn red carpet. I have inherited the great empire of CANCER! (*Beat*) Truth be told, I thought I would start crying, yelling, anything. I could not feel one single thing.... Because well, ... it just came to me that on the day when I had the genetic test, I mean the night before, I had packed a small suitcase. I knew that if the results matched my fear, I would go to Vienna... to have a preventive double mastectomy, since that was not practiced in my country. I had the fucking suitcase *ready*! I was not going to birth something, but to get rid of... a piece of meat... Ah, Vienna... waltz, schnitzel, apple strudel, and... double, preventive mastectomy.

> *The film ends here. She opens her purse, takes a lipstick out of a small mirror, and looks at herself with pride.*

GABBY: You see, when I came back from my ... *trip*, my colleagues found out. They begged me to take as much time as I needed to heal myself... and this was wonderful, but then I overheard them gossiping: "Yeah... double surgery.... She does not have breasts anymore. Yes, it is true. Is the procedure safe?

Is she sane? I do not know... I have never heard of this surgery.... Who removes their breasts *before* a diagnosis?" I joined them furtively, and then I screamed: DO YOU THINK THIS WAS ELECTIVE? IN MY CASE CANCER IS HEREDITARY. I AM A PREVIVOR!

> *She holds that jar in her hands. Drops it. An explosion is heard followed by darkness. When the lights return,* GABBY *starts to braid her hair. She holds a backpack. She takes a dress out of it. Puts it on. Takes out some headphones. Listens to music. Skips. Waves at someone.*

Scene Six

Recess

GABBY *and* TEDDY *are back to their younger selves. They browse through a Playboy.*

GABBY: These women... do they even know they are used?

TEDDY: They get paid.

GABBY: They should create a union... I mean. I'd never show my boobs and vagina for... how much do they get?

TEDDY: Plenty?

GABBY: Let's hurry. We are late. What's our plan?

TEDDY: When the teacher talks about the female body, we pull this out. (*Points to the magazine*) You make a scene. By now, everybody knows you have a big mouth.

As they talk, they do not notice that the teacher is behind.

AN ANATOMY TEACHER: Well, well, well. You must have been so absorbed in reading, if you did not hear the bell ringing.

TEDDY (*Startled*): Hello. We were on our way to the classroom.

AN ANATOMY TEACHER: Not so fast. (*Confiscates the magazine*) Explain yourselves.

GABBY: It came with the other newspaper you recommended to buy.

AN ANATOMY TEACHER: Do you think I was born yesterday?

GABBY (*Out-of-the-blue, just to distract him*): I read that elephants don't get cancer.

AN ANATOMY TEACHER: And that is relevant now because…?

GABBY: Because you teach science.

AN ANATOMY TEACHER: This (*points to Playboy*) is not *National Geographic*. Pff… elephants…

GABBY: Science cures our fears. Did you know…?

AN ANATOMY TEACHER: Enough!

GABBY: I read that all the bones in our body are connected, except the hyoid. (*Sticks her tongue out and makes fun of the teacher*) That's dope, right? That, plus the elephants.

AN ANATOMY TEACHER: One of these days you'd be sorry for your smartness. I'd find a way to *teach* you something about that tongue of yours... Inside the classroom. Now!

GABBY: Teach me what? That I can speak up my mind? (*Scoffs*) Teddy, let's go. We do not learn anything here.

They exit running. TEDDY *stops.*

TEDDY: Is it true?

GABBY: About?

TEDDY: Elephants.

GABBY: Yes. They have the zombie gene... According to a study, "...elephants have extra copies of two cancer-fighting genes: P53 hunts for cells with miscopied DNA, and *LIF6* obliterates the mutated cells before they can form a tumor."

TEDDY: We should have been elephants.

They continue to walk while projected we see various formulas, random Lewis' diagrams, a fetus inside an amniotic sac, etc. At one point, they stop to hug. As they try to part ways, they discover their noses have become elephants' trunks. They giggle.

Scene Seven

My Body Breaks in My Hands

TEDDY: Cancer is... (*A moment*) Cancer is a war with you and with others. Once a body breaks, you see your broken pieces scattered all over the house. Because you can't go out... not with a body that has betrayed you. You isolate yourself. You ask the same questions over and over again. When you are done with this phase, you feel exhausted....and snap at everyone. I am the first in my family to be diagnosed with breast cancer. My father even said, "You... *You*... Everybody laughs in our faces..." I have his eyes, the thickness of his hair ... I mean... used to... sort of... but ... cancer... look, in my case, it is *not* hereditary. Do you know what I hate more than cancer? Any cut, big or small.... I can't stand to see knives... or scalpels ... fuck, I can't even cut a loaf of bread. (*Stands up*) To cut a slice of bread.... Do you get what I'm saying? I'd rather bite into bread than cut it. (*Starts to run. Stops*) I used to be a professional athlete... I loved to reach the finish line and smile and take my shirt off and circle it triumphantly above my head.... (*Does that gesture, but fully clothed*) I started to run to get away from those bullies... they were making fun of me constantly. Then, I wanted to run to escape all sorts of realities... and I discovered that I was not even trying to run away from anyone or anything anymore. I discovered that I simply loved running. I was so good, I was selected to participate in local and national competitions. I came back with gold medals, and I was so proud to show them to my father... "Dad, look, *another* gold medal. Aren't you proud of me?" and he looked at the medal, throw it on the floor, and said, "Did they give you any money?" I wanted to run away... from my father. I looked with envy at the American athletes... they had everything. Great facilities to train in... I wanted to have what they had. I was rejected. I was told, "You should have come when you were younger. One-two more years, maximum, after which you'd retire... Sorry, but you are too old now to apply for an athletic scholarship." Then, boom, I got cancer. Statistically speaking, I was too young to get this disease. Statistically speaking, I am one of the few men who gets breast cancer. Damn it. Too old? Too young? First, I was fine paying for my treatments, then I was on a medical leave, but... my cancer was not fully cured... so, I pleaded with my bosses, they said, "No, you can't have an increase in your salary.... Based on what? That you have cancer?" They said they were not a charity. One day they left a message on my phone. They found a replacement... I was fired. I could not afford to pay for chemotherapy ... my rent... so, ...

> *Flashback.* A FATHER *enters. He does not face us during the entire scene. This is also cinematic. Like us,* TEDDY *is now a spectator.*

TEDDY: I do not know what else to do...Thank you for coming.

A FATHER (*Hands him an envelope*): Look, here, you have all you need.... You are the ideal candidate to get funds from them... read this carefully.

TEDDY: Thanks... but... (*hesitantly,*) is there, maybe, another way... are you ... sure? Absolutely sure???

A FATHER: I told you on the phone... I made myself clear. They claim they would help anyone who cannot afford treatment. They say the health of the patients is more important than (*air quotes*) some bills.

TEDDY: Why... I know... but tell me again... why are you doing this?

A FATHER: Because my daughter died. They (*points to the envelope*) kept postponing to send the payment to the hospital and those bastards were delaying treatment... I requested my daughter to be transferred to a hospital in Turkey... I made all the arrangements... all I needed was their signature... But they kept saying, "The money will be wired... Yes. Today." Today never happened.

TEDDY: You should denounce them publicly.

A FATHER: Got brain fog?! (*Changes his tone*): I had already filed a lawsuit against them... in fact, I should hear the sentence soon and, if that is not in my favor, I will continue my fight... **MY DAUGHTER IS DEAD! SAVE YOURSELF!**

A FATHER *exits. Flashback ends.*

TEDDY(*Repeats lines said before*): 2 full years. 24 months. 17,520 hours. 1,051,200 minutes. 630,072,000 seconds: cancer-cancer-cancer-cancer-cancer. So far.... I have paid ... (*Out of his pocket he takes a piece of paper that he unfolds very slowly*): MRIs, chemotherapy, mastectomy, prescription drugs, taking the train from where I live to go to the capital, hotel rooms, 25,000 euros.... Oh, listen to this. The state hospital did not have anything, except for free radiation, so I had to go to a private hospital... I mean, I could have done all of this for free in a state hospital, minus bribing the medical staff, but I'd have to put myself, ... (*Enraged*): LISTEN TO THIS: A patient who is trying to save their life is put on a ... waiting list. A fucking waiting list! My dad was making fun of me, "Last time when I had to stay in line and wait for something was during communism... We needed milk, so we woke up at 4 a.m. and waited for hours...I am not waiting in line to fix your boobs..." I was not waiting *in line*... like literally doing that... I was *on* a waiting list...

GABBY *enters somewhat triumphantly.*

GABBY: Turn the TV on! Your friend... he WON!

This moment is in V.O. The two of them hold hands.

"According to a documentary conducted by the Institute of Public Policies, it resulted that 'while some prescriptions fluctuate their price, for reasons that are mysterious to say the least, they eventually become unavailable. They *disappear* from the market. It appears that big companies when they see this trend, they calculate their loss. They say, 'Why should we make a deal with your hospital if the price that we negotiate first it is not honored? At the end of the day we lose money, and we risk to bankrupt our company... That's not worth it.'"

TEDDY (*To the audience*): Do you know what that *means*? Greedy managers renegotiate the price of drugs as they please, while *patients are placed cowardly on waiting lists*... That man's daughter is still dead... (*Skeptical*): He won...

> TEDDY *starts running. Returns. Hands* GABBY *an imaginary relay race baton.*

Scene Eight

These Wolves that My Skin Perspires

GABBY: One day... my sister was delirious because of her *metastatic* cancer. I had nothing to give her... they told us to take her home to die where she spent most of her life... they said, it was too late... I opened the door... she was crucified in that bed... it was August... so hot... and yet she was shivering... I caressed her body... I wanted to sing her a lullaby or something we both liked... as I approached, she was saying something... at first, I thought she noticed me... I thought she wanted to tell me something... she had not spoken in days... I was <u>so</u> happy... but she did not recognize me... She was delirious because of pain... she was saying something about some wolves... that were chasing her...

> *Projected, we see wolves which are running, hunting for food, eating, and then resting.*

GABBY: I asked, "Are you ok?" How in the world could she have been *okay*??? But we have no idea what to do, how to help sometimes... my sister was mumbling about some hungry wolves that were running after her... I touched her. Her skin was so dry. She could not move. She was in agony... I went to the hospital and demanded to have a nurse sent home... they said they were understaffed... they gave me a vial of morphine... and instructed me how to administer it to my sister... I was *not* a nurse... I came back home, I sang to my sister our favorite song, and poured morphine into her vein... to quiet her pain... to stop those chasing wolves... After she died, months after, I was watching a TV show on "Discovery" about wolves. I started to cry... I finally saw the wolves that were running after my sister... Funny how our brain works, right? I had goosebumps all over my skin... my sister's cancer was so advanced that those wolves were actually trying to eat her... to make her pain go away... taking her emaciated body away, too... and I found myself crying so hard, I heard a knock on my door. It was my neighbor. "Are you okay?" I collapsed in her arms. We went out... for drinks... I told her about my sister's cancer, my own genetic test, I told her to go back home, undress herself, and *touch every inch of her body...* call her doctor, ask for a mammogram... and *touch and love her body...* as we were deep into our talk, I see these two men approaching... one of them was a foreigner, he came as a foreign student, but when a civil war started in his country, he decided to stay ... learn our language...He had a beautiful accent... and I asked him to repeat what I was saying, and it was as if I was hearing the word cancer for the *first* time... because he was saying it differently... and I realized that this illness is always new... and we dive into the unknown every freaking single time... it is not our fault that our bodies break...

The scene with the wolves ends.

GABBY: I made *call after call after call*, and now... it's official: each person can have a mammogram. And the best part, it is FREE!

We see how everything turns pink. It lasts for a few seconds. Then, from above, we see a huge piñata in the shape of breasts. Right now, it has only made its presence. Nothing else.

Epilogue

One of Us

We are back in the hospital room, like in the beginning of the play. A neon is flickering. It will burn down during TEDDY's *monologue.*

TEDDY (*Tries to cover his mouth and nose*): Oh, my god... the smell... how much *chlorine* did they use today?! What was so serious to get rid of? Look, they took those posters off of the wall... they must have *cured* cancer. (*Beat*) Then why am I here?! (*On the phone*): Mom, are you paying attention? Please, sit down... Why? ... Because I've asked you, so...No, of course I know what day is today... Yes, it's my father's birthday. To come home? I'm coming. Am I late on purpose? No, I am not avoiding him. Are you sitting down? Yes? OK. My whole body is burning... I cannot take this *anymore*. WHY WOULD I LIE? TO AVOID SEEING DAD? Listen, mom... Mom, are you there? Forget the steak on the top stove. I AM BURNING! I should not have had chemotherapy... Who told me this? A team of oncologists from Germany... I sent my medical files there. What's next??? MOM, I LOST EVERYTHING, WHAT DO YOU MEAN WHAT'S NEXT?! What, there is always time? And if there isn't? What??? I'm young? SO??? I can still fight? *Never mind!* (*Drops the phone*)

> *He starts to undress. The atmosphere becomes more and more intense. Below his scar, we read the word "survivor."*

TEDDY(*Opens a window and, before he plunges into his own release from his **burning** body, says,*): Hippocrates, the Greek doctor... Do you know what he said? FIRST, DO NO HARM! Forget about all those pink and blue ribbons, races-for-cure, motivational posters. DO NO HARM! (*Devastated,*): Like anyone cares. Hippocrates is dead, too.

> TEDDY *is about to jump. When, all of a sudden, he is drenched in chlorine. He starts to laugh so loudly, the walls of the hospital collapse and we are in an open space.*

A CIVILIAN: A change of clothes! *Now!* This human is shivering. (*Realizing the smell,*): *Chlorine*?!

> *He touches* TEDDY *gently. He comforts him. Takes off his own shirt and puts it on* TEDDY. *Sees the scar; sees the word "survivor." Embraces* TEDDY *very tight. Everything in the background turns into snowdrops. Like in the previous scene, in V.O.: "Cancer kills 140 Romanians daily and the disease is diagnosed late, according to data presented by the Federation of Cancer Patients Association (FABC). The lack of information & screening programs is the main cause for the late detection of the disease. The top forms of cancer are pulmonary and breast. The Federation also called for a National Oncology Plan, which would help change things. Such a plan should cover screening programs, access to investigations, novel therapies and genetic tests, which would lead to personalized treatments. A National Oncology Register is also needed, the Federation said. In 2018, Romania recorded 83,461 new cases and*

50,902 cancer deaths, according to Globocan data (Globocan Cancer Observatory). The federation said many of these deaths could have been avoided if a strategy to fight the disease was in place. A report, published in the European Oncology Journal in 2013, showed that the number of cancer deaths doubled in Romania from 2009 to 2018."

GABBY *enters. She starts to hit the piñata.* TEDDY *waits for his turn.* A CIVILIAN *invites the public to participate.*

END OF PLAY

Endnotes:
1. For the definition of a hospital: Art. 1: Ordinul nr. 914/2006 (In Romanian)
2. For information about elephants not getting cancer: https://www.sciencemag.org/news/2018/08/elephants-rarely-get-cancer-thanks-zombie-gene
3. About the hyoid: https://www.livescience.com/7468-hyoid-bone-changed-history.html
4. About poor managerial decisions in Romania's medical system: https://www.ipp.ro/lipsa-de-medicamente/ (In Romanian)
5. Info about the artwork: https://www.youtube.com/watch?v=JPDM7psNkYQ
6. About pain: https://www.change-pain.com/grt-changepainportal/change_pain_home/chronic_pain/insight/definition/en_EN/298801001.jsp
7. Breast definition: http://www.sfatulmedicului.ro/dictionar-medical/san_4416 (In Romanian)
8. Yoko Ono's *Freedom*: https://www.youtube.com/watch?v=G7-egx5ke8w

9. The final quote: https://www.romania-insider.com/140-romanians-die-of-cancer-daily (In Romanian)

Post Scriptum:

Snowdrops and Chlorine is both a play about cancer sufferers, with plenty of juicy material for actors to sink their teeth into, and an educational document. It is dedicated to Florescu's mother, who died of breast cancer in 1992. The author says, "Ultimately, my goal is to fight for implementing a mandatory screening program, as well as to expose the utter futility of products designed to raise awareness for 'breast cancer.'"

Among the misperceptions the play exposes is the assumption by many people (including me) that breast cancer is a female disease, that men don't get it. Here, however, the first breast cancer patient we see is a man, Teddy, a physical education instructor and former sprint champion, who perceives the disease as a betrayal of his masculinity, his very nature. We follow him as he sinks deeper into denial and despair.

Another character is a woman, Gabby, who is a lawyer working on a malpractice case where a doctor misinformed her client about cancer. Gabby gets a diagnosis that says there is a 90% likelihood she will develop breast cancer, based on her physicality and the fact that her family has a history of breast cancer. An *aggressively* proactive character, she travels to Vienna to get a preventive double mastectomy, which is not available in Romania. She remains strong herself, and tries to encourage her dear friend Teddy, whose father ridicules him for being "a loser" with "a feminine disease."

There are four other characters, all played by the same actor, a husband who has lost his wife to the disease; a middle school anatomy teacher who has a hard time trying to explain female anatomy to his wise-cracking pupils, teenage Gabby and Teddy in flashbacks, a father who has lost his daughter because of the inadequacies of the bureaucratic health care system; and a civilian who can easily be someone from the audience. So far, so good; there are powerful speeches about breast cancer and the intellectual and emotional reactions to it. But what will give this piece real theatrical power happens right in the middle of it. A character "named" Eleonor, a cancer survivor, testifies for five minutes or so about her own story; then the play is stopped and the houselights brought up, for a 10-minute dialogue with the author, the director, at least one breast cancer survivor, a family member who has been affected indirectly by the illness, and the public. This will obviously be different at every performance, may also include "drama therapists, doctors, navigators, nutritionists, pathologists" and will be amplified by projected images.

It is Ms. Florescu's hope that such public education, especially in a theatre-loving country like Romania, may open public discussion, empower cancer patients, and perhaps educate the health care community. But even in the US, with all our pink ribbons and cancer awareness events, this play can have a powerful impact, for it is when we see and hear the human reactions of patients that our own human connection is called forth – statements like these: "My body has wounds." "My wife was now cancer-free, but could not get pregnant." "This is *not* my body!" ",,a body that has betrayed you." And "I was fired. I could not afford to pay for chemotherapy."

There is hard information in this piece, such as, "Cancer kills 140 Romanians daily . . . the disease is diagnosed late, mainly because of a] lack of information & screening programs." But there is also something that only theatre can do; the actors' live presence and skills set before us the human dimension of the disease as we see their reactions, and the final shock of Teddy's (attempted) suicide is both tragic and a (failed) *coup de theatre*.

Teddy is still alive. Now, what?! -- **Christopher Hirschmann Brandt**, Actor, educator, director, Medicine Show Theatre

When I read Catalina's play, I had just come out of a Midwestern medical theater with my husband who went through a double coronary bypass surgery in June 2020, as soon as COVID-19 rules allowed "elective" procedures. Still running like a fast cave river under my consciousness is the thought that I *could have* become a widow. At 46 years of age, a vegetarian, non-smoker, and athlete, my husband was the "image of health," as his cardiologist wrote bafflingly in his medical file. Now, the expression has become a running joke in our family, as we look at present and future with a different perspective. The hardest part to watch of the instructional YouTube videos is the opening of the thoracic cavity, the invasion of the sacred wholesomeness of the body, so well described by Paul Kalanithi in his book *When Breath Becomes Air*. We avoided death by luck and circumstance. His scar runs from the top of his sternum to the bottom. We call it "the zipper."

Unknown to Catalina, everything in her play spoke to me deeply: physical decline, scars, breath-taking pain, vulnerability, trauma, suffering, sadness, and isolation. As far as diseases go, breast cancer is physiologically and emotionally different from a heart attack, but their possible outcome – death – is equally serious. Breast cancer affects both men and women, and yet we don't hear men's stories often enough.

Teddy, the male cancer survivor in the play, is the "image of health," a fitness instructor and former sprint champion, blindsided by distorted cellular processes inside his body. As cancer researcher Candace Pert reminds us, "[i]t's a fact that every one of us has a number of tiny cancerous tumors growing in our bodies at every moment." As Gabor Maté explains in his book, *When the Body Says No,* in cancer, the process of apoptosis, the physiologically regulated death that ensures healthy tissue turnover, is distorted. Cancer starts with cellular death and birth gone wrong.

One thing that the oncological treatments rarely inquire about but Florescu's play does is giving us a glimpse into the character's family systems and relationships. We get to learn what is going on in their lives. Teddy's sadness is fueled by life events: being bullied, loved conditionally by his father, and rejected by schools for being too old for a track scholarship. Gabby's sister died of breast cancer, and the story of her decline is deeply poetic and touching in its detail (In an interview, Catalina spoke candidly that the wolves were not randomly chosen, that her own mother, close to death, had mentioned them incoherently.)

The sensitive yet blunt description of her sister's last days reminded me of the experience of reading *How We Die – Reflections on Life's Final Chapter* by Sherwin Nuland. At the end of the play and this book, the viewer/reader is no longer reticent to contemplate one's own demise. Interestingly, Teddy's character describes the impact of cancer at the micro-level or individual suffering, while Gabby's character asks the audacious, macro-level questions: *"What kind of country is that where there are no national screening programs, where hospitals do not have treatments, and where we dismiss someone because they are not at risk? What kind of society prefers to wait for a diagnosis rather than seek to implement prevention?"*
In the face of systemic issues such as insurmountable costs of cancer treatments, or lack of access to screening, an individual may wonder: Does my country care if I die? The play reminds us that assumptions about our value are at the heart of every rule and piece of legislation.

Time is of the essence in cancer, especially when it comes to diagnosis and treatment. With a cancer diagnosis comes a shortened future. As Gabby says in Fourth Scene, "[t]hat woman had a future, now her family has a past". Since March this year (2020, A.N.), thousands of cancer patients have not been able to continue chemotherapy due to COVID-19. As the world slows down to negotiate social isolation and the search for a vaccine, cancer advances inside bodies until distorted cellular death and birth eventually becomes an all-silencing death.

For many people, this is a year of sickness, loss and grief. Through the tyrannical character of the anatomy teacher, Florescu's play suggests that death can install itself also at the level of dialogue, when voices and questions go unheard or unanswered. He instructs and punishes through shame and avoids open conversations and inquiry. The anatomy teacher (of all people!) chooses discursive closure *("Quiet down!", "Get out")*, rather than listening and asking questions. The tumors of failed conversations grow in front of our eyes as students and teacher talk in parallel streams, unable to connect.

Catalina Florescu's play is a call to action to implement free screening programs, to reverse the market mechanisms that encourage pharmaceutical companies to withdraw cancer drugs from the market simply because they don't make money, and to listen better. She invites the public to debate why spend millions of dollars on marketing events and merchandise such as pink ribbons, when that money could be invested in free screening programs for men and women without health insurance. Fourth Scene starts with "Your Honor…", because a legal authority has to lay down a new law and new rules, and that is no easy task.

Snowdrops and Chlorine is therefore quite timely with its stated goal of increasing awareness, access to free screening programs and affordable treatments for breast cancer sufferers. It also brings the artistic accomplishment of stirring viewers' emotions, of *bothering* them, of making them feel worried, anxious, defying, and sad along with the characters. The dialogue flows naturally, the energy of the cursing is sharp and swift, as in real life. The spectator is sensorially stimulated with projected images (theater-in-theater, or rather *life*-in-theater), live dialogues with cancer victims, changes in scenery, contexts (hospital, classroom, court), pace and rhythm.

This is a play where audience members who are also cancer patients or caregivers can see their struggle on stage, and even participate in it. They will find their experiences expressed in the characters' anxiety and fears, in their resilience and desperation for how the medical theater confronts them with its combination of miraculous medical achievements, bewildering diagnoses, high financial costs, omissions and misinformation (see the story of the husband in Third Scene – *Grief*), and sometimes gendered or patronizing messages.

Viewers who live with cancer will feel heard, seen, and understood. The mid- and post-performance dialogue and testimonies add even more value to the artistic production, whose format is remarkably nimble and adaptable to both Zoom or stage performances. Catalina's activist theater is an innovative, creative, and collaborative way of stimulating dialogue on how the world deals with breast cancer– **Dr. Elena Gabor**, Associate Professor of Communication, Bradley University

Within the relatively short text of the play, I encountered numerous aspects of experiences familiar to me through my previous work as program director at Gilda's Club Chicago, a Cancer Support Community. First, the falsely idealized image of man and masculinity is shattered by a reality: male breast cancer. The audience experiences this when introduced to Teddy as he smashes his reflection in the mirror. Second, the dangers of misinformation and ignorance: The second scene, *Back to School*, explores the need to challenge any embarrassment around biological differences in service of health education. How can children learn about health when even the instructor is not comfortable discussing anatomy? Gabby challenges the instructor's self-denial of his own embarrassment with health information she received from the school nurse.

In order to live our daily lives, most of us engage in a certain amount of denial. Otherwise, no one would want to leave their front doors for fear of random, harmful events. No one wants to be diagnosed with breast cancer either, but we must negotiate with our denial in favor of mammogram screenings to increase treatment success and early detection. Accurate health information encouraging annual screenings with appropriate referral allows us to confront our ignorance and to benefit from taking appropriate action. Furthermore, the right information at the right time is important in reducing patient stress. The importance of this is reflected in the matter of Gabby's court case in the fourth scene.

The third scene, *Grief,* also emphasizes patients needing the right information at the right time. Oncofertility addresses the reproductive needs of patients prior to starting chemotherapy. Sperm banking and egg retrieval are now topics that are discussed with patients prior to beginning chemotherapy to avoid the grief experienced, for example, by the couple in Catalina's play who were not given the opportunity to make *informed* decisions prior to the wife beginning chemotherapy.

Cancer may create strong feelings of loneliness and isolation for the person who is diagnosed. Family members and friends may be supportive by offering rides to chemotherapy, delivering cooked meals, or simply by being a lifeline to the world outside of hospital visits. Despite everyone working together, that sense of loneliness can be pervasive for the person in treatment. *Snowdrops and Chlorine* masterfully relates this experience to the audience through the aesthetic distance created in the opening scene. The characters and audience are together, while each remains separate.

Snowdrops and Chlorine is an effective vehicle allowing the audience to experience an array of issues related to cancer firsthand. Awakening minds to the challenges cancer presents is a step towards addressing those challenges. The hope inspired by the survivors' stories is a healing balm to encourage us to meet those challenges. If cancer smashes the picture we had of life, anyone impacted by it (friends, family, and patients/survivors) would find a shard of that experience captured in this play. Catalina Florina Florescu holds a mirror up for us to see the inequities and we quickly achieve clarity on our way to empowerment -- **Rebecca Fritz**, LCSW, JD

Appendix

Personally, in this never-ending cancer "puzzle," one of the most rewarding experiences has been to talk to patients & to find out about their struggles and strategies for coping with pain. Over the decades, I have met so many beautiful survivors who taught me how to open up. For this volume, I interviewed three of them: Rebecca Pine, Catherine Guthrie, and Michael Singer.

It has become more and more evident to me that we do not know how to talk about what hurts. I was in contact with the editor-in-chief at LIBERTATEA, an important mainstream Romanian newspaper, because I wanted to make sure that my research and goals would become available in translation to Romanians, too. I knew Catalin Tolontan was one of the journalists who wanted to shed light on the massive corruption within the medical system in Romania and make sure his investigative journalism would lead to expose those crass abuses of power. Helped by several whistle blowers, his effort was then continued by Alexander Nanau who worked on his critically acclaimed documentary *Collective* – Romania's first double nomination at the Oscars.

I knew that the subject of breast cancer would be provocative, to say the least. Helped by journalist Andrada Lautaru, I was able to share these interviews (below), as well as talk about my plays, and, to my surprise, have a Romanian breast cancer survivor finally share her perspective.

Questions

1. In 150-200 words, please speak a little bit about yourself (e.g., where were you born, what are your hobbies, what do you do, what was your favorite childhood meal?)

2. How did you find out about breast cancer and what followed immediately?

3. In choosing to go flat, what was your biggest frustration, but also what was your most rewarding victory?

4. In Romania, many women die because of breast cancer because they are diagnosed very late, when cancer is too advanced. One of the huge problems women have is that they do not know how (and are also not encouraged) <u>to embrace their intimacy</u>. More exactly, they are **afraid** to undress to show their breasts for a regular annual check-up. Based on your experience, what would you teach women in Romania regarding opening up, learning how to care for their lives/bodies and minds? How would you encourage them to get over this unhealthy taboo, and go see a doctor?

5. Finally, please finish this thought: "*Dear* breast cancer, ………."

Answers
Rebecca's:
1. I was born in Morristown, New Jersey, U.S.A. While growing up, I enjoyed writing, riding my bicycle, climbing trees, and wading in the little creek that ran behind my street.

2. I had my first mammogram when I was 30 because we have a strong family history of breast cancer. My second mammogram at age 33 revealed irregularities that turned out to be cancerous. I learned that I carry the BRCA1 gene. I had five "second opinions" and was surprised to hear that each doctor recommended a double mastectomy with reconstruction and removal of my ovaries. I decided to have a single mastectomy with a saline implant. Before my second (prophylactic) mastectomy, I was able to have a daughter and breastfeed with my remaining breast.

3. As I prepared for my upcoming surgery, I knew I didn't want another implant. Researching other options, I decided I would rather go flat than have extensive flap surgery. I felt it wasn't worth the risks of surgical complications and infection. I was frustrated that I could only find one photograph of a young woman without reconstruction. Having a visual reference point is incredibly helpful when making life-altering decisions. Creating more visual representation was also one of the driving forces behind "The Breast and the Sea," a project I co-founded with photographer Miana Jun. We offer seaside workshops for breast cancer survivors, previvors, and patients, focusing on inner healing and self-acceptance. Participants experience support, movement and photographic practices, thus, witnessing with scars bared in and around the water. It has been a tremendous gift to be able to hold space for those going through, surviving from, and living with the effects of breast cancer and to share tools to help empower them as they heal. To learn more, please visit https://www.thebreastandthesea.com/. I have become an advocate for the option to "go flat" after mastectomy because reconstruction is often presented as the only surgical result. I have bared my scars on national and international media in the hopes of helping to normalize our post-cancer bodies. I facilitate a breast cancer support group and offer regular

workshops and programs focusing on healing through writing, art, and nature. (https://www.rebeccapine.com/)

4. There have been many cases of breast cancer in my family. There are two common responses to fear of cancer risk: ignore it or become proactive. I have seen the results of each response up close and personal. My cousin didn't have regular breast screenings. Even after she found a lump in her breast she waited many months before going to the doctor and seeking care. I saw her condition worsen and watched her rapidly decline. Sadly, she died way too young. My mother, on the other hand, was very proactive with her medical care. When she found a lump, she was evaluated and began treatment promptly. She went on to live fully upon recovery. There are no guarantees in life, to be sure. I believe that knowledge is power. It stinks to have a high genetic predisposition for cancer, but KNOWING about it is a blessing because then I was able to make empowering choices based on that knowledge. I decided to follow my mother's example. My breast cancer was caught early and fortunately has not recurred. I chose to have risk-reducing surgery by having a mastectomy instead of lumpectomy, and prophylactic removal of my unaffected breast and ovaries four years after cancer. I highly encourage all women to perform monthly breast self-exams and yearly breast exams by their doctors (and more often if there are any breast changes or possible changes in between visits). I understand that baring our breasts is vulnerable...but it is an essential part of self-care. Our lives matter! Delaying screening can mean the difference between cancer being caught early or progressing to advanced states. Unfortunately, sticking our heads in the sand and hoping it will not happen will not prevent this disease from occurring! I think of breast self-exams much as I think about flossing my teeth - it's a necessary part of looking after our bodies to make sure that they are functioning optimally and that our lives will be as comfortable and long as possible!

5. Dear breast cancer...I would never wish you upon another human being. I would also never have expected to find such support and community among those who have shared this diagnosis with me. I never expected the ways large and small that my life has changed since my diagnosis, or how healing it has been for me personally to support others struggling with cancer, to give back. Without my experience of cancer, I wonder if I would have become as comfortable with myself, my body, and my feelings. Although I have lost my breasts, I feel more whole than I have felt at any other time in my life before.

Catherine's:
1. I grew up in Louisville, Kentucky. I'm a women's health journalist and the author of *FLAT: Reclaiming My Body from Breast Cancer*. My hobbies are cooking, yoga, and reading.

2. I discovered my breast cancer in January 2009 when I rolled over in bed one morning and felt what seemed like a bruise on the upper part of my breast. After a mammogram, a diagnosis, and genetic testing, I underwent a double mastectomy with no reconstruction five weeks later.

3. In choosing to go flat, my biggest frustration...
Going flat felt like the least barbaric of my options. Because I have a small frame the only reconstructive choice given to me at the time was the Latissimus dorsi flap, which meant severing my back muscle, tunneling it under my arm, and laying it over a breast implant. My other breast was small, so the surgeon advised me to get an implant on that side too, for symmetry. He said most women just wanted to look normal in clothes.
I want parity. I want surgeons to present the option to go flat with the same energy, acceptance, and enthusiasm that they present reconstruction. I want surgeons to stop assuming they know what women want and what's best for women.

4. I would encourage women to think about what words they might use to convince their sister, daughter, or best friend to see a doctor if they found a lump. Most likely, they would encourage that person to seek medical attention because they love that person and want them to take care of themselves and live a long life! Sometimes we have a hard time following our own advice or giving ourselves the loving messages we give other people. Seeking medical care is a form of self-love and self-care.

5. Dear Breast Cancer...you don't define me.

Michael's:
1. My name is Michael and I was born in the Bronx, one of the 5 boroughs of New York City. I went to Bronx Community College and majored in Electrical Technology. After working several jobs, I started working for the United States Postal Service as an electronic technician. I spent 31 years with the Postal Service and retired as a Facilities Maintenance Manager. I got married to my beautiful wife Patty, my childhood sweetheart, at the age of 25, and we have been married for 35 years. I like to ride my motorcycle, camp, fish and cook. My favorite meals are pizza, pasta, and barbecued meats. I got diagnosed with male breast cancer at the age of 50. I had no idea men could get breast cancer, even after I *lost* my sister two years before to metastatic breast cancer.

2. This December (2020, A.N.) I will be a 10-year survivor of breast cancer. I am a male who was diagnosed at age 50 with ductal carcinoma in situ. As a male, I never checked myself and ignored the issues I was having for several months until I went for a routine exam and mentioned this issue to my doctor. Within days I had a needle biopsy followed by a surgical biopsy and finally a full mastectomy of my left breast. I was shocked and embarrassed at the same time, as I had never heard of men getting breast cancer. Even after my diagnosis and surgery I was

still ashamed and called it "chest cancer" when I was questioned. I tried researching male breast cancer back in 2010 after my diagnosis and there was little to no information, and no one male to reach out to. One day I saw a *Special* on The Katie Couric TV Show; her guest was a man named Brett Miller, who was a young male breast cancer survivor. This changed my life as I was able to finally connect with other men with breast cancer. I reached out to "The Brett Miller 1T Foundation," "Male Breast Cancer Coalition" and have been an active member since then participating in getting the word out, i.e., that men can get breast cancer, *too*. I also avail myself to other male breast cancer patients if they want to talk about this as I have first-hand knowledge of what it is like. I have had the opportunity to serve as a consumer reviewer to evaluate research applications submitted to the Breast Cancer Research Program (BCRP) sponsored by the Department of Defense. It was at one of these programs that I had learned about the National Breast Cancer Coalition and about its specific training called "Project Lead." This educational program teaches policy-setting and decision-making roles of breast cancer research advocacy and focuses on the basic language and concepts of molecular biology, genetics, clinical trials, epidemiology, research methods and advocacy. I knew this training would benefit me in my continuing to spread the word on male breast cancer and help educate the public to this disease that is killing men due to the lack of education and the late stages of breast cancer when they finally become aware. Since my retirement and my shocking diagnosis of male breast cancer, I have been participating in as many breast cancer events that I could have possibly, spreading the word about male breast cancer.

3. Yes, most men go flat, but there are some that have reconstruction with tattooed nipples. This is a personal choice for men and women.

4.This year alone (2020, A.N.), in the United States 2,620 men will be diagnosed with breast cancer and approximately 500 of those men will die due to the later stages of their diagnosis. Done be embarrassed like I was in the beginning, hiding it from everyone! I know it takes courage as we are considered the 1% of breast cancer, but we all have breast tissue and can get breast cancer. Some of us might be genetically pre-disposed and carry this genetic mutation passed on from their mother or father, some might get it from the environment, or some might just develop it due to other factors. But all men should know the early warning signs like women are taught. Men should know how to do a self-breast exam and if they don't want to touch themselves have a doctor or a significant other do this for them. Having this knowledge and talking about it could save yours or a family member or a friend's *life*. If you go to the www.malebreastcancercoalition.org, there are videos on how to do a self-breast exam in many languages.

5.Dear breast cancer, thank you for introducing me to so many amazing men and women since my diagnosis, but you have to make yourself more treatable to my friends and families with metastatic cancer. I am sad to have lost so many of these relationships. Just make yourself a chronic disease that is treatable and not deadly!

CANCER, CHOREOGRAPHED

CANCER, CHOREOGRAPHED

Synopsis & history:

This is my third and last piece in **Staging Breast Cancer Trilogy**. As noticed, *Mia* revolves heavily around femininity on account of mastectomy, reconstruction/going flat, and infertility. *Snowdrops and Chlorine* reminds all people that breast cancer can be diagnosed both in male and female identified bodies. With that notion acknowledged, the play's focus is mostly technical (i.e., some medical jargon), as well as targeted towards the cost to fix our broken or about to break bodies. Finally, *Cancer, Choreographed* is an experiment because it is not about acting lines, but instead a visual immersion, as well as a dance to which we are all invited to participate.

As I reach the end of this trilogy and I edit it during the longest year of our lives (because of the pandemic, which is still not over), I know that our bodies are the best narrators we will ever possess. Sometimes, our bodies tell stories using words; daily, however, they are our kinetic force reminding us of the energy that comes from within, as well as from interacting with others. Therefore, I want the trilogy to end with a dance. Even when a body crawls in pain, a dance may become an interior monologue. Pain is never static. Our reaction to it is fluctuating, to say the least. My advice? Listen to your body carefully. Take ample time.

Industry praises:

I found this game of hypostasis, of attempts to escape from the dark or haunting universe of illness, interesting. It is also fascinating that Catalina does not try to materialize cancer as a precise figure. There are, however, the breasts on a plate – a surreal image, yet a necessarily blunt one to help the audience remember why the show is teaching: always more than "just" about a diagnosis. The multimedia side seems to act as an organizer of the dramatic universes and this is what makes it possible to create quick escapades from one universe to another, from the hospital in the desert, or on the seaside back to the operating room. In short, this medium is of paramount importance to give rhythm and dynamism to the performance. The rhythm is established through the rapid changes of scenery using the projected images. Obviously, the projected images will have to be well thought out and designed, integrated with the dance and the dramatic situations, however symbolic they may be – **Liviu Dospinescu**, PhD, Professor of Theatre, Université Laval, Quebec, Canada

Five minutes into the show and the dancers must tell the audience and only through movements the story, which they will see unfolding in the next hour or so. It's like an overture in opera. When I read Catalina's script, the concept of the Japanese art of kintsugi, "golden joinery," came to mind. As a pottery is made whole after its parts broke, so does the human body: it needs to be rebuilt after being invaded by the destruction brought by erratic cancer cells. The stage is full of black panels, which can get different forms throughout the show. There are projections on these panels, or the choir can draw with chalk what the male character sees through the telescope. The choir of the ten women forecasts, explains, and solves dilemmas. It's like a choir from the Greek tragedies, but the tragedy is cancer. If in the beginning of the show the movements are very well controlled, sharp, and clear, as they go along, they must degrade and become rattled. Here I'm talking about the *tango* that everyone dances. Maybe at the end of the show the audience will play with the dancers and dance with syncopated movements – **Ioan Ardelean**, PhD, Associate Professor, University of Arts Tirgu-Mures, Romania

Characters:

MAN
A CHORUS OF TEN WOMEN

Time & Place:

We could be back to ancient Egypt when the first case of breast cancer was diagnosed, or we could be in our present time. In other words, unlike other plays, here time is just an ... accessory.

Note on characters:

MAN is nameless. He could be in his late 50's. His body is not full of muscles like a fitness fanatic might be. In fact, it is the body of a man who is an epicurean. He likes to eat and drink. Or he used to. He does not seem to enjoy physical activity too much. He likes to sit and observe the world. His clothes are plain, but his type is not. Play as much as you'd like with that statement.

A CHORUS OF TEN WOMEN: The numeral is not randomly chosen. It is the first double-digit number. The idea of double and of symmetry plays a fundamental role, not only here, but also throughout my trilogy. Age-wise, these women could and should be as varied as possible. In terms of clothing, follow instructions as presented below (whenever they are available). If it is possible, extend the call to all types of bodies, i.e., ideally do not limit this performance to body-abled ones.

Note on music:

Except for Maurice Ravel's *Bolero* and Shigeru Umebayashi's "Main Theme" from *Onmyoji*, this piece is ready to accept any suggestions. If directors/choreographers want to ask those in the audience to choose a piece or two on the spot, to make their presence count while assuming there are imperfections (that is, the choreographed movement may not align perfectly with a song/music), I will be fine with that choice, too. I feel that this last piece in the trilogy should be the most flexible and collective of all.

Scene 1

The only verbal indication of the dance appears in V.O.: "I'm sorry, you have advanced breast cancer." The statement can be repeated until it fades away, or it can be said only once.

We see MAN whose back faces us. He is getting ready to look through his telescope. He has a cup of tea next to him. He wears a robe. He flips through a magazine. He checks his phone. The bright artificial light is progressively replaced by darkness and the celestial show. We see what he sees (and that is open for interpretation). The sky is full of stars. We are far away from a polluted area. The scene ends with MAN seated in the same position as in the beginning. That means that at one point he stood up, attempted to dance, while the stars stayed on the sky, or they slowly disappeared. Towards the end of the scene, he does not move at all; instead, he makes sounds that suggest he is mesmerized by the stars, while at the same time, he points to something that is damaged in his body and needs to be healed.

Scene 2

We see MAN. This scene seems to be a repeat of the first one. Maybe it even is. Until we hear a loud noise. For a second, we think it's related to the weather. And in part we are right. We see projected a series of mammatus clouds, known to bring thunderstorms or tornados. Made out primarily of ice, in translation mammatus means "mammary." We stay on this selection of images and sounds for a few minutes (2-3 maximum). MAN holds an ice cube in his hands. He dances with it while the ice melts. He slips.

Scene 3

For a few seconds we do not realize what has happened to MAN. We see A CHORUS OF TEN WOMEN dancing while holding a plate on their hands, upon their heads, etc. Their choreography is very precise. In fact, this dance feels like a march. In the background, we see projected images from mammograms and breast ultrasounds. Many scalpels are dropped. Whatever was shown in the previous scenes, i.e., the sky's show, that is now replaced by these black and white images of our bodies' interiors, more exactly our breasts and armpit areas as illuminated via mammograms and ultrasounds. A CHORUS OF TEN WOMEN gets closer and closer to us. As that happens in a very synchronized fashion, the black and white images as projected become multiplied like in a kaleidoscope. It is increasingly chaotic. The women stop dancing. The music stops. The images stop being projected. The women invite us to eat. Or, so it seems. Allow yourselves to be tricked. Yes, A CHORUS OF TEN WOMEN holds breasts on a plate similar to Francisco de Zurbarán's 17th century painting *Saint Agatha*, the patron saint of breast cancer patients. Then, transition to Thedra Cullar-Ledford's 21st century *Platters*.

Scene 4

A CHORUS OF TEN WOMEN recedes and, as they do that, they become smaller and smaller, maybe their bodies resemble a constellation. They dance to reveal that MAN is on an operating table. He is alone and bandaged. He stares at the ceiling. The neon light seems to make MAN react in terror. He closes his eyes. The women return. They create a circle around him. They do not hold anything in their hands, but sway their bodies gently, back and forth, back and forth...

Scene 5

...until their movement transports us outside of that hospital. We are on a beach. It is night. The waves touch the women's ankles.

They giggle. They dance playing with water. MAN does not move. The women start to take the gauze off and clean his body. They lift him off of that operating table, now turned into a hospital bed. He seems to be like a dummy, a puppet, something without agency, because he cannot have control over his bodily movements. A CHORUS OF TEN WOMEN does not give up. They help MAN dance and coordinate his moves.

Scene 6

It's winter. It's snowing. Everything is covered in white. It is beautiful and peaceful. We are swiftly moved from the whiteness of the snow to the whiteness of a hospital. The women are dressed in white, too. They dance and, as they dance, they undress themselves. They will not be naked. Imagine this moment similar to wearing a medical/hospital gown and underneath it everyday clothes. The suggestion is that these women would like to return to their lives prior to their having entered a hospital. Whatever they may be wearing should be *very* colorful. The whole white room is brought back to life and that is also expressed by their moves. That is, if in the beginning their bodies suggested the pain after a major surgery and/or aggressive treatments, towards the end of this scene they dance a very difficult dance that is indicative of the resilience of the body, including the one in agonizing pain. I'd assume that a body starts to "dance" internally when it is faced with this kind of prolonged, debilitating pain.

A CHORUS OF TEN WOMEN ends the dance by extending their hands. I'd suggest they hold clay or play dough. They raise their hands in front of their faces, but, as they do that in synch, they stop around the breast and then armpit areas as if scanning over their skin with what they have in their hands. Eventually, they cover their faces. We see projected *Venus of Hohle Fels*. This is assumed to be the earliest sculptural depiction of humans via this medium. The sculpture fits in our hands. This indicates how much we should protect our bodies.

Scene 7

A CHORUS OF TEN WOMEN is lined up in a single file fashion. MAN is wheeled on stage in a rather brutal gesture (*Imagine someone offstage who pushes his wheelchair carelessly*). The women start to dance by keeping their formation. They are mechanical. One by one they exit the stage, each with a short, memorable *signature* dance (of no more than 2 minutes). MAN looks at them with satisfaction. There is now only one woman left on stage. She gets closer to MAN. She dances next to him. At first, she is shy, but becomes increasingly more and more provocative. As we see the movement intensifying, like in Maurice Ravel's *Bolero*, an explosion is heard. Everything is dark. When the light returns, MAN and this woman stand up. They face each other. They start to dance a tango.

Scene 8: Infinite, or LOVE

The other women return, and they dance a tango, too. Since now this is an odd number, one of them may join those in the audience or stay on stage. She watches the show, but I expect her to stand up and either dance with a made-up partner, or get very close to those dancing. The dancers' movement transitions so that we see how they line up, facing us this time. They sway their bodies. MAN breaks this formation and starts to dance by himself. The rhythm is soothing. The stage is immersed in stars. A CHORUS OF TEN WOMEN watches MAN and then, slowly, they join him. They continue to dance, however, the lights in the theater indicate the show is over (*i.e., they become brighter and brighter*). The spectators may be invited by ushers to join the dancers on stage, or to leave. There is a mix that is intentionally unscripted.

Try to leave this final moment as organic as possible. After all, regardless of how educated we are, how much this illness has scarred us, we almost never know how to react *properly* when we hear: "I'm sorry, you have (advanced) breast cancer."

END OF PLAY
END OF TRILOGY

<u>Post Scriptum</u>:

I love the concept of *Cancer, Choreographed* with all invited to participate at the end. We all find new meanings through movement. Inviting the participation from the audience will keep the art alive and ever changing. Moreover, focusing on a man with breast cancer will help to dismiss the notion that breast cancer only happens to women. The 10 women are our ushers while the man is the focus. My only suggestion is to add something about the man to your title. It will provoke a question to learn more – **Dr. Jill Bargonetti**, Breast Cancer Researcher, Hunter College

AFTERWORD

When Laurie Brown Kindred asked me if I wanted to be part of her "Moms We Lost because of Breast Cancer" series from her podcast BAD RIGHT BREAST, I said yes immediately. I knew that I could talk about my mother any second of any day. But when I told my maternal aunt, who is a doctor, about the interview, she said: "Will you speak about your mother's father's sister, too?" "What? Who?" "Lenuta died because of breast cancer." "What????" I had no idea. I asked my sister. She said, "Yes, I knew... Why are you digging in the past?"

It is very hard to talk to my sister about our late mother even now, 29 years after she died. Why didn't I know about this? Or is it possible that I was told, and somehow managed to block this information?! I was 17 when I lost my mother and until her very last days I was in denial. My sister was 20 when our mother died. She came from Bucharest where she was studying as an undergraduate student to be there with us. I was still in high school. I was constantly reminded to go to school, to learn, to finish my senior year because I would have big exams coming up (i.e., baccalaureate and admission to college). On the other hand, my sister was in the house almost constantly. Did she find out about our mother's aunt who died then, while I was out?

In this photo, my maternal grandpa and his sister have one of those very rare moments of going to a photo studio to create a memory. On the back of the photo, in Romanian, Lenuta wrote: "I do not feel well." She was diagnosed in her late 20's, had surgery, and died within a year. My mother knew about this tragic event from hearsay.

Up until this "discovery," I thought the reason why my mother refused to undergo surgery was because she did not want to have such an invasive procedure that would imply losing a breast. In her bedroom, she had a copy after *Nud la malul marii* by Nicolae Grigorescu. One day, as I entered the room, I saw my mother looking at the painting. She loved the arts, so I thought she was just looking at the image. More, she had this copy even before the diagnosis, so, in the moment, everything seemed fine. However, now, I taste my mother's desperation and it feels like a blow to my stomach.

You can Google the image and then picture this: a daughter, a mother, a wife, a woman in her 40's knows she has breast cancer. She remembers a "story" about her aunt who died because of this illness. She holds a copy after a painting in which a woman is depicted naked, enjoying the sun by a seashore. Her breasts appear to be in perfect health. My mother holds this painting close to her chest and, although she is fully dressed, she must have felt naked, betrayed, and scared.

As for me? I put myself back in this picture of loss and, since I can't have access to my mother's medical record (therefore, I have no idea what type of breast cancer she had), I keep doing my monthly self-exams and wait to have my annual mammogram.

When I heard about this aunt, I felt numb. When I do not feel numb, I want to yell. For 29 years I kept tormenting myself by saying, "If only she had surgery... if only she did..." and I am so angry. Because I had no idea how terrified she must have been thinking that surgery would be an added painful experience resulting in her premature death (like her own aunt's).

What do I want to say exactly? <u>That each cancer is different</u>. That no one should go through this diagnosis and treatments alone. That it helps to talk, to investigate, to ask questions, to reassure the other that we are there for them then and there, rather than to type an ending to a trilogy. Loss and regret have such a perverse and unremovable taste. If possible, avoid it for the longest time.

About the photographer of the trilogy's cover image (in her own words):

Jamie Shombert is a photographer/artist born and raised in New Jersey. When she was diagnosed with breast cancer, she picked up her camera. She knew immediately she was going to document her progress from start to finish, wherever that "finish line" would be. From the very first photograph she had no interest in producing sanitized – or what she called "pink washed" – work. In her mind, this would be a disservice, not only to her own experience, but also to other patients, spouses, and families who would one day face a diagnosis of their own. Cancer is a brutal disease and Jamie wanted to acknowledge that brutality through her artwork. She proceeded to produce a body of work that encapsulated chaos, fear, and helplessness – a quite often-overlooked part of the breast cancer experience. Jamie's other work has been shown at Arts on Division Street Somerville, NJ; Guild of Creative Art Shrewsbury, NJ, and Alfa Art Gallery, New Brunswick, NJ.

About the author:
Dr. Catalina Florina Florescu was born in Romania and came to the States in 1998. At Purdue University she met four wonderful professors, each with a different specialization who encouraged her to research and write a dissertation in the field of Medical Humanities, an interdisciplinary program that combines her love for the palliative arts with her curiosity about scientific discoveries. Catalina has a son who is passionate about music and biomechanical engineering. She teaches at Pace University and she is the curator for New Play festival at Jersey City Theater Center. She has published and/or edited 8 books, and works on her **exit** book, *Female Playwrights and Intersectionality in Contemporary Romanian Theater* (Routledge). More about her here: http://www.catalinaflorescu.com/

About my *beloved* mom: Rodica Georgescu, here a teen, loved the occult, music, the visual arts, and all things transporting her outside of this world. When my mother was very sick, my sister paused her undergraduate experience and came back from Bucharest to nurse our mother. In a reversed Pietà motif, Mari washed our mother's emaciating, deeply marked by cancer body. My grandma birthed only one child whom she lost too soon. My role model, my father, joined mother in my childhood bed so she would not die alone. I wrote this trilogy to share my painful story and diligent research. While I still long and I will uninterruptedly be longing for my mother's touch, nonetheless she smiles so fully in this photo. To *feel* her, I listen to my mom's favorite piece of music: "Radetzky March" by Johann Strauss. Thank you for reading this trilogy.

www.ingramcontent.com/pod-product-compliance
Lightning Source LLC
Chambersburg PA
CBHW022115040426
42450CB00006B/718